The College Selection Compass:
Helping Families Navigate a Difficult Course

Susan P. Nichols and Rebecca J. Callow

iUniverse, Inc.
New York Bloomington

We would like to dedicate this book to our families for their patience, guidance, experiences, and advice. We appreciate and love you all.

Acknowledging help when one finishes a book is always easy. The only hard part is the fear that you forget to thank someone or notate a source. As we composed and researched this book, we spoke with over fifteen hundred students, parents, teachers, and administrators from numerous high schools and colleges. We want to thank everyone who took time from their busy schedules to share their knowledge and expertise with us. Colleges that were particularly helpful, by allowing us to survey their students (listed in alphabetical order) are as follows: Lewis & Clark College, Miami University, Middlebury College, Ohio State University, Ohio Wesleyan University, Regis College, Tufts University, The University of Oregon at Eugene, Wheaton College, and Willamette University. We thank each of them for sharing their campuses and students with us.

We also want to encourage your feedback, whether positive or negative, and have listed our emails for you to contact us if you would like. The strength of this book is its readers and the experiences they have. Thank you to everyone who has helped us this far. Thanks to you, our readers, for any help in the future. Rebecca Callow (adcallowjr@ aol.com) and Susan Nichols (nichols.ma@aol.com).

The College Selection Compass:
Helping Families Navigate a Difficult Course

Copyright holder: Susan P. Nichols and Rebecca J. Callow
Copyright Year: 2008

iUniverse books may be ordered through booksellers or by contacting:

iUniverse
2021 Pine Lake Road, Suite 100
Lincoln, NE 68512
www.iuniverse.com
1-800-Authors (1-800-288-4677)

ISBN: 978-0-595-49192-6 (pbk)
ISBN: 978-0-595-61000-6 (ebk)

Printed in the United States of America

Contents

Introduction

Welcome to *The College Selection Compass*. You have our support! It is our sincere hope that, based on our own experiences and the information we have gathered, examined, and organized, we can help you as a family during the time when you are thinking about, looking at, applying to, and deciding on colleges. Whether your daughter or son is interested in a small school or large university, a rural environment or a city setting, it is our goal to help you to figure out how to fit the right school with the right individual—and maintain communication, parent to child and child to parent, along the way. As you may already know, that is no small task! Trust us: we've been there.

We want to acknowledge here as well that at times it's not the parents who work through the process with their children. It may very well be a sibling, grandparent, aunt, uncle, teacher, or family friend who takes on the role of parent when a teenager starts the college search process. For the sake of streamlining the labeling of the different support systems surrounding students, however, we will continue to use the terminology of parent, with the utmost respect given to other family members or friends who may be an integral part of many students' college searches.

A generation or two ago, attending college was an entirely different experience than it is today. The fact that this book interests you to begin with shows that your family assumes someone in your household will attend college. High school students today face an onslaught of pressures, at an increasingly early age, from their parents, their high schools, their peers, and a multitude of colleges. Just fifteen years ago, most students waited until spring of their junior year in high school to visit colleges and begin thinking about campus choices. At many schools, it is now common to see freshmen and sophomores attending tours and information sessions along with the proverbial juniors. Students and their parents seem to want to start the "college process" earlier and earlier in an effort to gain more knowledge, see more schools, and make final decisions about which colleges to apply to and whether or not to file early applications. To be sure, many teenage schedules demand these early visits, and students with special interests outside of academics find that they have to assert themselves with coaches, musicians, and professors in order to showcase their special talents. It seems evident, however, that there is an ever increasing pressure on students and their families to earn a spot at "the perfect college" while each student or family may not understand how to go about finding the ultimate match. This conundrum is made even more difficult by the typical difficulties parents and teens have discussing important issues.

Further complications arise if either the parent or the teen does not feel a particular level of importance when considering the search process. Too often the parents are eager to organize the process from A to Z while the teenager has little or no sense of immediacy about the issues at hand. Conversely, there are also many students who want to work completely independently without parental or professional input.

Let us be honest with you here. Between the two of us, we have six children. Three of them have graduated from college. Two of them attend college presently, and the last one, bless her soul, is wading through college visits as we write this. We've had one who applied early to the college of his choice and was deferred. We've had one who went off to his favorite school only to transfer after freshman year. One son swore he needed to attend college in a different time zone, only to spend four years twelve miles away from home. One daughter embraced the college of her choice only to need a leave of absence for a medical condition before returning to campus. Another daughter couldn't wait to get to college, but found out she was more homesick than any of us had ever thought possible. In admitting all this to you, we are trying to tell you that even under the best circumstances, with the most excellent planning, most carefully constructed road trips, and ample parental and school support, there are no guarantees of an easy road through the college process. Experiences, students, locations, programs, and unforeseen circumstances can alter the best laid plans for any student or family.

We have found, however, first in our own families and now from our research with students, high school counselors, college administrators, and our own colleagues, that parents and students *can* work together discussing all the ins and outs of college choices. As parents, as families, we can't control the outward paths the college process will take. We can, however, at least work toward finding ways to help control the way we deal with the process as parents, teenagers, and families as a whole. The more families communicate openly and honestly, the more positive their experience will be. The proportion of the 1500 students we polled who said they appreciated parental support, and in retrospect would have liked more—71 percent—showed us we were on the right path. Only 16 percent of students felt that their parents were too invested in the process and wished they had had more independence (see graph 4).

We want to give you some bricks-and-mortar ideas in this book that we hope will help you think about interesting college choices, organize meaningful college visits, and learn sensible techniques for keeping track of college information, from tests and scholarships to academics and career planning, not to mention sports, theater, music, and club activities. Our ultimate goal, however, is to go beyond the bricks and mortar on these pages and give you some ideas to help you honestly and openly communicate as a family along the way. If college applications have to be postmarked in twenty-four hours, the latest movie can wait until after the postal deadline: the student has to be realistic. If the applicant has five days to e-mail the basketball coach concerning the exact time for the student-coach interview, the parent should not ask about that particular e-mail on day one, two, three, or four of that time frame. As a parent, try to share as much information as you can, but remember—your son or daughter may not have your specific comfort level.

Although we have gained a depth of knowledge from our own experiences, it's important for you to know that we spent almost two years obtaining permission to solicit information from colleges in the Northeast, on the West Coast, and in the Ohio Valley. We personally interviewed over fifteen hundred college students from forty-eight states and all ethnic backgrounds. The range of schools they attended included single-sex and coed small colleges as well as public and private universities, including Ivy League schools and one of the largest institutions in the country. Permission was hard to obtain from administrators because they are fiercely respectful of the privacy of their student populations. When we gained acceptance from a college or university, however, we were always impressed with the enthusiasm the students showed. They were quick to share their experiences and worked diligently on our questionnaire. The statistics we were able to glean from their answers were extremely helpful not only in proving a number of facts that we had already suspected to be true, but also in affirming what the twenty-first-century high school student has experienced, for better *or* worse. As the college students continually showed us, they have many different experiences but many similar feelings.

You're navigating uncharted waters, whether this is your first experience or your last. Each child is different, each college search is different, and each year college applications are different. Our goal is to help you plot a course for a successful journey. Our personal experiences as well as our research have given us insight we think you might like to have. Our hope is that we can help your whole family make the most appropriate choices. Now take a deep breath. We're with you all the way.

1
Begin at the Beginning

It was the best of times; it was the worst of times…
—Charles Dickens, *a Tale of Two Cities*

Question: "What would have helped to make the college search and application process less stressful?"

Answer: "Knowing what I know now. But that's impossible. The stress was necessary and integral to the process."
—College student

As silly as this may sound, if you are the parent of a college-bound student, try to decide on a simple way to begin discussing the whole college process with your teenager. Your son or daughter may attend a high school where the guidance department is very college-oriented, setting guidelines and organizing meetings for parents and students to start the college wheels rolling. If this is the case, don't feel you need to accelerate the process by taking road trips to faraway campuses or sending for information from your old alma mater. Guidance counselors are professionals who should have their fingers on the pulse of the college application process and should be guiding you and your teenager through the process, from the administration of the PSAT (Preliminary Scholastic Assessment Test) or its equivalent to making sure that complete applications have been mailed on time or submitted online by certain specified dates. In other words, your son or daughter's guidance counselor is a good start. Make an appointment at the end of the sophomore year or the beginning of the junior year. Especially if you are beginning this process with your oldest child, it will be helpful to have a guidance counselor to map out general guidelines for you to digest. Your son or daughter may have specific needs or talents that will require extra attention or organization, and the guidance counselor may be helpful in pointing out appropriate options. Meetings like these generally work best without your teenager in attendance, partly because she or he may have shown absolutely no interest as yet, and partly because you may have some concerns or specific questions that you would like to address with the counselor before the process begins.

Once you have met with the counselor, and perhaps discussed the meeting with your son or daughter, the counselor could in turn meet privately with your teenager and explore some possible college choices. Remember, however, this is still early to be making any serious decisions. Most students and parents at this point don't have a great deal of information with which to make decisions. It is important to note that the students we polled who felt they visited an adequate number of colleges before applying were more likely to have started thinking about the process before their junior year. Students who wished they had visited more schools tended to start the college search process later (see graphs 2, 3, and 5). Statistically, 31 percent of those who felt they had visited the right number of colleges started discussing the process with their counselor in the first half of their junior year. Not surprisingly, 28 percent of those who wished they had seen *more* colleges didn't start discussing their plans with their counselors until senior year, and in this same category, 40 percent of those students didn't start visiting colleges until their senior year.

Once you have scheduled the guidance office meeting, schedule a meeting with your teenager. Share what you have learned and ask him or her to share with you. Give this meeting a name—College Voyage, Part 1, or something that can be referred to at future times. Obviously this is a serious step, but if you can bring a little levity to the situation, it will create a positive feeling and create an open atmosphere. Try to schedule this meeting over a meal or at a time when each of you can focus on each other and the task at hand with minimal distractions. Be sure you each share what you've learned, but as the parent, be sure to share only what you learned from that particular meeting. A long diatribe on the blizzard you drove through with your dad on your first college visit in upstate New York or the sit-in you witnessed at the campus you and your best friend stayed at are not relevant at this time (or probably at any time in the future as far as your teenager is concerned) and will waste precious minutes with your teen at a time when new information will help each of you.

This is also a perfect time to set up some ground rules for meeting together as a group. Pick at least two or three specific meeting dates and times over the next few weeks (remembering that dinner time may be best for everyone). If you are juggling a schedule that involves younger children, try to make other plans for them. Hire a sitter if possible, or look to friends or relatives to help out. It is more important than you may know at this point to carve out some undivided time with your teen. These meetings enable you to commit to the whole experience, and arranging individual time to work through the college decision and admission process will make all aspects of it easier in the long run. We found in our research that 71.4 percent of students noted that, in retrospect, they were glad that their parents devoted time to them. Some students, approximately 12 percent, even stated that they wished their parents had spent *more* time with them. This statistic varied quite significantly by region, however, with 23.5 percent of students in the mountain states wishing that their parents had been more involved, while only 4.1 percent of mid-Atlantic students felt the same way (see graph 18).

Many aspects of the tasks before you may govern your meetings, but try to see each meeting as an opportunity to communicate with each other, and try to stay focused on the college issues before you. Keep labeling each meeting to keep track of your progress (College Voyage, Part 2, etc.). Your teen will find plenty of time to figure out ways to stay out beyond curfew on Saturday night. Your job is to use your college meetings *only* for college "talk." Each meeting can start with a quick review of what has already been accomplished. Try to allow as much time for your teen to talk and organize things as you can. If parents take over the meetings, then the purpose of the meeting becomes blurred. Remember, your daughter or son is the key player here. Try to step back and be a sounding board as well as an organizational aide. Don't hesitate to jot down notes as you are meeting—questions and praise can be meted out as well as added ideas. A well-known psychiatrist and author, William Glasser, penned some interesting statistics that we offer to you here:

We learn…
10 percent of what we read
20 percent of what we hear
30 percent of what we see
50 percent of what we see and hear
70 percent of what we discuss
80 percent of what we experience
95 percent of what we teach others .

After you have all reviewed what has been accomplished, see if any of you have any further thoughts on past discussions. If you have visited a few more schools since your last meeting, if national test scores have been made available, or if your teen has met with a counselor, coach, teacher, or mentor, make some new additions to your information and discuss their value. Figure out if any follow-up is required, and then look toward what you need to do before your next meeting together. Remember that at this stage, your teen can take advantage of online college information and tours. The tours are frequently a good way for teens to see the differences between college campuses, especially concerning academic expectations, size, location, graduate programs, and extracurricular activities including sports. Schools and public libraries make computers available to students who don't have access to them at home, so be sure to look into these possibilities if you aren't online at home. They can visit these colleges on the Web without you looking over their shoulders, but encourage them to jot down some information on each college they visit so they will remember the schools. They can also use the notes for making comparisons to other colleges.

Unfortunately, many high school guidance offices are unable to provide useful services to students regarding colleges. These guidance offices are overwhelmed with high school programs that keep counselors busy with scheduling and special programs; there are simply not enough hours in the day for counselors to provide needed assistance to students and their college applications. Even the busiest counselors are generally very good at watching deadlines and seeing that recommendations are filed, but searching out the best colleges for each student may be something outside their time frames.

Try to talk to other parents whose children have gone through your child's school system, but make an appointment with the guidance counselor regardless. If you determine that your school cannot provide the services you feel you need, then take the information you are able to get from them and begin your own additional work with your teenager. Organized and planned family meetings are even more important if guidance offices are unable to give optimal help. Try to think of this as an opportunity to explore new horizons with your teen. Whether you are a single parent or one with a spouse, a grandparent or a legal guardian, this can be a time of discovery with your teenager, a time to explore openly and honestly what it will take to go the next step. The process is daunting and evokes not only the physical feelings of stress, anxiety, and frustration, but also the emotions of helplessness and fear of change. Try to embrace the challenge in its entirety, remembering that the more knowledge you acquire, the easier it will be to feel you are making the right decisions.

Staying organized throughout this process is a monumental task, but we have come up with some ideas that will help. Buy a two- or three-inch loose-leaf notebook and dividers. We found that this enabled us to alphabetize the schools we began to think about and visit, through actual visits or online, and place any information we received in its own space. This notebook should serve as an integral part of the meetings you will schedule with your teen. Keep it in a place where you can all access it. It's okay for you as well as your teen to put ideas or information in the book. You may want to flag your information with a post-it or similar marker so that your teen has an opportunity to see it. As you move forward in the process, you may want to buy a plastic file box in which you can store any college information that comes in the mail, is pulled offline, or is provided by the high school. Separate folders for each school in the plastic file box will augment the notebook. One of our most inventive daughters put tape and a marker in her file box so that she could notate and tape business cards of professors, coaches, and admissions professionals to the folders she had for each college. It was a terrific way to keep the business cards from getting misplaced, and with e-mails on most business cards, she could reconnect with any of the college personnel whenever she wanted to, whether to ask a question or get an update.

At this point in the process, you should each have a sense of getting organized and be learning that many possibilities and opportunities await your teen. If you have established a relationship with the high school guidance counselor, scheduled several family organizational meetings, learned how to contact colleges and universities online, and at least visited a few campuses, even in an informal way, you have made a great start. Keep the lines of communication open, but try not to question your son or daughter more than necessary, remembering that each child has his or her tolerance level—as do you! There may be a sense of increased stress as the process goes on, but open communication with your teen will lead to positive feelings for all of you.

2
Honest Questions, Honest Answers Concerning School Choices

What's it going to be then, eh?
—Anthony Burgess, *A Clockwork Orange*

Students and parents need to be realistic about college choices. They need to take a good, hard look at the kinds of schools that are appropriate. There are so many choices, and students, parents, and professionals often forget to "look outside the box." "Safety schools" and "reaches" are terms we use all the time. Peel back the onion and continue looking for something new and intriguing on the college horizon. Maybe a different school will feel like a great fit, maybe it won't, but give it a try. What do you realistically have to lose?
—High school guidance department director

Once you have established the firm foundation explained in the last chapter, you can begin to move forward regarding college choices. By now you have met with your son or daughter's high school guidance counselor and checked out online, or actually visited several college campuses. You have worked out meeting times together, organized a notebook, and perhaps even bought a plastic file box with folders, scissors, and tape. These things vary in importance, but all of them provide ways for you to communicate with each other as well as keep the process organized. Many of your future decisions regarding college visits, applications, and choices will rely on having completed these initial steps, so try to accomplish them before moving on.

As we've suggested before, each time you meet, review what you have already accomplished, check on any deadlines that might be looming, and figure out what else you want to accomplish in the time you have together. If your teen hasn't drawn up a list of potential colleges to look at (online or in person), try at least to get started on a group of potential schools. The guidance counselor may also have created a list for your teen or mentioned some choices that are worth exploring. This is an excellent time to begin taking a hard look at the kinds of schools in which your son or daughter is interested. Most students are still unsure of their future career paths, so it is certainly wise to explore several different types of schools. Remember that academics, location, size, financial aid options, and extracurricular interests should all be considered for each school on the list.

Looking at a small liberal arts college in a rural area is not a good use of your time if your daughter is a devoted artist who wants to live in the city. On the other hand, a large university with huge Division I athletic programs may not be a realistic choice for your son who quarterbacks his small-town football team. Many high school athletes, even those who are recruited, try out or start to play their sport at the college they are attending only to find out that the athletic commitment is overwhelming, their athletic abilities don't meet the coach's expectations, they get injured, or they simply do not enjoy the team schedule or dynamics. Even with a coach's assurance, sometimes the student-athlete doesn't find the sport or the expectations to be what he or she has assumed they would be. An athlete must assume that college sports all too frequently take more time than high school sports. Remember that almost all athletes who play college sports do so because they are extremely skilled at them. They are probably used to starting each game and playing significant roles in team victories. It can be difficult for high school athletes to make the transition from high school sports to college competition, so do not fall into the trap of choosing a school specifically because of one coach or one sport. Counselors and coaches often use the "broken leg theory": would you still like the college if you broke your leg and couldn't play your sport? Keep that point in mind when looking at extracurricular programs in the colleges. You are still looking at colleges in general, so don't let one program or coach sway your decisions yet.

For the student who has a specific academic passion and skill, there are professors at many colleges who specialize in one subject or another, and matching the student and professor to academic interests is an ideal way to connect with a school. A well-known ornithologist in Ohio teaches at a small college, but he draws students from various sections of the country who spend parts of each academic year as well as the summers working on papers, field work, presentations, and grants, enriching their educations far beyond a typical classroom course. An environmentalist at one of the state schools in Oregon has pioneered some findings on climate change. Her students share her long-term vision of a more "green" America, and she's always on the look-out for new students who are eager to study with her.

It is clear that the academic piece of college applications is supremely important. Specific academic skills, interests, and passions can augment the typical college application and enrich any student's college experience. Don't hesitate to explore the possibility of connecting with a particular department or professor at colleges. Sit in on a class, make an appointment with a professor, or work with a special high school teacher to find the colleges that offer special academic interests and highly qualified professors. Just like coaches and advisors, professors may have an in with college admissions offices, and their support of a candidate can be surprisingly important. Teens need to celebrate their accomplishments and interests and not be afraid to establish multiple connections at any of the colleges they are considering. The relationships they cultivate during the college search process will enrich their experiences and help them make decisions when the time comes.

Be sure, however, to keep your options open at this point. You don't want to cross any types of schools off your list simply because you don't like the name or the size; instead, you need to locate schools that will fulfill your son or daughter's academic needs and abilities as well as other aspects particular to each individual. You can always add or delete schools from your list at any time, so don't be shy about looking at schools that *could* be a good fit. This is where online searching can be a great asset. It's impersonal enough that you won't feel you're asking a "stupid question" when you look for information. It is, however, an excellent way to discover things about schools, from academic achievements and school statistics to sports teams, choir schedules, and on-campus clubs. You can acquire e-mails through online campus services, too, so your teen could e-mail a professor regarding a certain course of study, a coach concerning a team, or an advisor about a club. The responses your teen receives may reveal a great deal about a certain school and its personnel.

Often, a college connection through e-mail will result in the coach, professor, or advisor referring you to students, assistant coaches, or teaching assistants to enrich your knowledge and bring more answers to your questions. A number of colleges now have times when you can go online and ask students there any questions that you may have. This is another way your teen can find out interesting facts about a college that he or she might not have felt comfortable asking in a large tour group or with parents present.

It's also important to remember that there are things we think are important about colleges, and there are things our teens think are important about colleges; many of those concerns may be very different, so don't hesitate to do your own looking online.

Most teens, simply because of their age, interest level, and experience, may not take as much advantage of the virtual college tour as they might. You as a parent can take the same virtual college tour and discover a plethora of information your teen may not have found. Presumably, you know much of what interests your teen, so if the school has a highly renowned math department and your daughter has finished her high school math requirements with no thought of visiting higher math, then let that part of the tour go and click to another department or course of study you think might interest her.

You may also want to research graduation and transfer statistics and perhaps even new construction on campus. One of our daughters was very taken with a campus she visited, but she loves working in libraries, and this outstanding school had a surprisingly antiquated library. The college that she eventually chose has a brand new library. Now she spends many hours nestled into her favorite upstairs corner while still finding other areas that are ideal for group work. No one thing should draw a student to a campus, but parents and students alike should be sure to see the value of academic departments and extracurricular programs, and the physical buildings (including any new construction or plans) should be noted by both students and parents.

Things as mundane as distances from airports, bus depots, and railway stations are amazingly easy to determine and will be helpful for all students and their families. Public transportation, via subway in city areas or shuttle buses on more rural campuses, is important for most students. Some campuses even sponsor bike programs where any student can use a specific kind and color of bike to travel from one area to another.

College calendars and campus events are clearly found on these web pages as well, so if you're in close proximity to a campus, take advantage of the opportunity to watch a play, a choral production, a guest lecturer, or an athletic event. This will give each of you the opportunity not only to see the talent and camaraderie of the students, but also how the student population supports its own community.

Another way to add to your list of possible college choices is to match students' national test scores (PSAT, SAT, ACT) to the range that colleges' test scores have published. Some colleges have cutoff numbers and will not even consider a student whose test scores are below a certain number. On the other hand, some colleges don't require reporting national test scores at all, so a student might consider learning about those schools to see if any are of particular interest. Maximizing the range of schools adds new possibilities and combinations of college choices.

All of the information garnered in this initial forum can be invaluable in discussions at your prearranged meetings. The more actual and virtual tours you have been on, the easier your comparisons will be to make. With each tour and each meeting, try to keep in mind that tours are not yet campus competitions, but rather campus comparisons. You may have found academic departments and extracurricular activities you're excited about in a city you won't consider. Don't be discouraged; just keep looking at schools in general and what interests you specifically. Always keep in mind, both parent and teen, that there is not one perfect school for you. There are many wonderful choices.

3
Where Do We Go From Here? Planning College Visits

Now what I want is facts.
— Charles Dickens, *Hard Times*

Be a sounding board for your child and a glorified travel agent.
— College admissions representative

This chapter combines everything we have covered so far. Parents and teens need to take a good look at what they have learned and how they can connect their knowledge to organizing some college visits. You know what many colleges offer and why your teen wants to look at them, but you need to figure out what to emphasize for each visit and what each institution has to offer. Take or retake stock of what the initial concepts were and see if you need to make changes. Your goal is to achieve a great match between student and college. Students and parents alike must avoid being seduced by the prestige of an institution or its size, location, extracurricular activities, or student body. There are so many factors involved in finding the best schools for each teen that it is important to continually evaluate where you are in the process. It's time to build a reasonable list of colleges, probably a number between six and ten: two you are sure you will gain admittance to, two or three that are good possibilities, and two or three that are stretches. Some students will apply to more schools for a variety of reasons, usually because of the Common Application, or because they feel more secure submitting more applications. This is definitely up to you as a family, but it does not guarantee more acceptances in March or April. This is also a good time for each teenager to evaluate the process to date and set aside some time with parents, a mentor, a guidance counselor, or a teacher to plot out the next stage of the college process and college visits.

Your first college "visits" may have been the drive-through version while you were at a local campus, on a family vacation, or visiting friends in another state. Hopefully, whether you took a tour, stopped and explored the campus and some of its building, or didn't even get out of the car, those visits provided some important background for your next round of visits. This is when you may want to review your lists of what you are looking for in a college. Taking the time to prepare for college visits ahead of time will prevent you from wasting your time on campuses that don't fit your needs. Don't limit your visits, however, to just one type of school. Big-city schools, state universities, and colleges with several campuses can offer many courses of study or opportunities that small city or rural colleges cannot access. Keep an open mind about various schools as long as you can since the number of schools you see online as well as on campus will continue to help you decide which colleges interest you the most.

The more surveys we tabulated, and the more colleges we visited nationwide, the more we found that the *number* of schools students visited was very important. Of the college students who said that they wished they had visited more colleges before applying, an astounding 82.5 percent visited fewer than five. The 59.9 percent who said they visited the "right" number, however, also visited fewer than five while 33.1 percent saw six to ten, and 7 percent saw eleven or more. Of the students who wished they had visited more schools, 37.8 percent said that the pressure of the college search was overwhelming or very difficult (see graphs 11 and 12). These students also found parental pressure and filling out applications to be very difficult for them. It seems that the more secure the student is in seeing numerous campuses, the less stressful the whole process is. Only 26.6 percent of those who visited the "right" number felt that parental pressure and filling out applications were more difficult.

Students who saw what they considered the right number of schools were clearly more content with the choice they made; they felt certain that the college they were attending was right for them. This was true whether students had applied ED1, ED2, or followed standard admissions guidelines (see graph 19).

If you have a school vacation coming up, see if you can schedule some college visits. Most schools, even if students play a varsity sport, will carve out several days of vacation when there will be no high school activities, and students are encouraged to visit colleges at those times. If you know your school runs this kind of schedule, try to make your plans early. Map out a course of colleges and universities that interest you and make plane and hotel reservations if necessary. Even learning about the different parts of the country can be fascinating if you embrace the process. Colorado's mountains are nothing like New England's even though the weather can be similar, and the California and Oregon coasts bring their own interests and weather patterns that are very different from the Midwest or South.

Well before these organized visits, be sure that your teens have prepared any information they want professors, coaches, or administrators to know about them. It's highly unlikely a coach or professor will be able to talk to a student who drops in for a visit or an interview. The world of recruiting students, whether for academics, sports, theater, or music continues to be increasingly organized and competitive, and it is in all students' best interest to send letters ahead of time to anyone they want to see on any of the campuses they are going to visit. Don't forget that this also sends a message to the professionals the students want to talk to: these students are organized, interested, and capable, definitely qualities college professionals have come to expect. There are sample forms at the end of chapter 8 that you should feel free to use as guides. They can be altered to fit the student, college, and area of interest, and they are something to seriously consider if your teen is looking to pursue a specific interest at the college level.

If it is next to impossible for you to get away for college visits during the school year, try to take some time to visit campuses near to you. Most cities have good college programs, and teens can visit one or two schools in a day with friends or family. If teens go by themselves, encourage them to acquire and save as much information on paper as they can garner since it's hard to remember everything from several campuses, especially if they're with their friends when they are touring the colleges. There may also be campuses that you and your teen can visit after a school practice or a game. If a school is only a few hours away, and you can get a noontime start, give the visit a try. Often, there are information sessions and tours in the mid-afternoon, and you can certainly see how a campus operates in the afternoon through the early evening. In actuality, more seems to go on later in the day when the students are in class or engaged in activities. There are many early mornings when the nine a.m. college tour seems to have the largest crowd walking around campus!

Once you return from visits, be sure to take the time to organize your materials. As difficult as it may feel to process what you have culled from your campus tour, trust us: you don't want your hard work ending up at the bottom of a miscellaneous pile in the kitchen! Put information packets, course selection booklets, extracurricular information, and anything else you have accrued into the folders or notebooks you have already organized. If you have a long drive, try to get your teens to write down their feelings—whether positive or negative—about the campuses, tours, students, professors, coaches, or anything else that will keep each college visit separate and memorable. The more you can get done within twenty-four hours of your visits, the clearer they will remain.

Don't forget to write a thank-you note to anyone you spoke with personally. They have set aside important time for you, so reward them. Whether you had a formal interview with an admissions officer or an informal meeting with a student, a thank-you note establishes you as someone who truly cares about the school, which can give you an edge in the admissions process. Some people suggest using e-mail, but we don't. Establishing e-mail contact is always easy and usually a great way to communicate informally, but don't sell a quality thank-you note short, particularly if you want to impress a professional.

The process may begin to feel long and involved at this point, especially if you're juggling other children's schedules and your own work. Try to feel empowered by all that you have already accomplished, and don't be discouraged if much of what you have learned is negative information. Even if you and your teen have not found a large number of interesting schools so far, your knowledge base is constantly increasing, and when you find the kinds of schools your teen is interested in, you will be that much more experienced. Everything you are learning has value. Keep that in mind at all times.

4

Stress and Deadlines: Hold Your Course Steady

In times of stress, the best thing we can do for each other is to listen with our ears and our hearts and to be assured that our questions are just as important as our answers.
—Fred Rogers, *The World According to Mister Rogers*

I feel so much pressure as a parent, and I know she feels tremendous pressure as a student. She wants to make all the "right" choices, but she's not sure what they are, and I don't really know how to help her.
—Parent of a high school junior

Some of the most difficult issues are still before you, not the least of which is getting a bearing on where you stand with your teen concerning college choices. What are you expecting from your teen at this point? What is he or she expecting of you? If your son or daughter avoids college discussions and expresses little interest in the college search process, then try to save your conversations for your official meetings. For whatever reason, some teens feel that all adults they come in contact with have only college on their minds. Regardless of how often or rarely you bring up the topic, they feel that you're thinking of nothing else. In fairness, your teen is quite right. The world surrounding your teen is loaded with advertisements, mailings, and well-meaning adults all trying to figure out how the proverbial senior will fill his or her time after high school. By senior year, many English teachers include college essays in their curriculum. Their intent is to help the students, but it makes some students feel they can't escape the pressures of the college application process. Guidance counselors frequently send notes and make appointments to meet with students. All students need to ask for teacher recommendations, as well; the reality is that the earlier they request recommendations, the better.

One can see that by senior year, even a skeletal list of things to do during the college application process can easily feel overwhelming to the typical high school student, who is already coping with day-to-day social issues and academic requirements as well as extracurricular activities. Your teens may feel frustrated rather than excited, and it's important to respect their feelings, whether or not you think they are valid. Filling out college applications was clearly the most stressful part of the process for all the students we polled. Over 42 percent of them described it as somewhat overwhelming and challenging (see graph #6).

Try to step back, and as we said before, save your college discussions for your official meetings. If you have them regularly scheduled, and you keep track of questions or points you want to raise, then you will be respecting your teen and meeting your college goals at the same time. Obviously there are deadlines that must be met and videos, tapes, or résumés that must be written, but all these issues truly can wait until your scheduled meeting times. Remember that if you write down goals for the next meeting at the end of each meeting, then you can see if those goals are met, and then go on to ask your teen where to go from there or bring up your own questions, results, and goals. During the meeting, it is you, the parents, who can emphasize the importance of deadlines and time issues. Our teens are rarely as tuned in to dates and time frames as we, their parents, are. We mention in the "Nuts and Bolts" chapter the advantage of making some sort of timeline, whether it is an actual horizontal line with specific dates and deadlines, or a calendar or a computer model that you construct on your own. Any kind of timeline helps both students and parents plan ahead for deadlines. Any tools you use prevent a last-minute rush that always creates more potential problems than necessary. We cannot stress enough the importance of organization. Each organizational function you can complete, together or separately, will continue to help you down the road. Even if you duplicate some deadlines and dates here and there, each time you see things on a checklist or in a notebook, you will be that much further ahead organizationally.

If you have a teen who is enthusiastic about discussing the college process or brings up questions, concerns, or interests outside of the established meeting times, try to make time, *right then*, for him or her. Those are often the "teachable" moments for both parent and child. We have been constantly amazed in talking to college students by the varied perceptions they have regarding the college process. Any discussion regarding colleges, whether positive or negative, will add to the depth of the information you have. Teens may want to discuss what they learned on a virtual tour, or may have heard something at school that needs clarification. They're probably not going to talk to you about the typical weekends on college campuses they are interested in, but they may want to compare something in the college's acceptance requirements or whether the basketball team has ever played in the NCAAs. If you don't know the answer to a specific question, that's okay. Tell your teens you'll find out the answer and then follow through. It would be ideal to do the detective work together, but if time is a factor, then it is wise for you to offer to find answers to their questions.

Try using online college resources to find answers; in this way you can show your teen the answer and maybe something else interesting about the school you happen across on its Web site. Specific offices, representing academic departments, athletics, music, drama, religion, or community service departments, frequently have office assistants who can either answer your questions or put you in touch with people who can. If you call them and get an answering machine, be sure to leave a message including the best way to reach you. The speed and accuracy with which your call is returned may tell you even more about the school you're calling than you have anticipated. A response that includes the information you seek within a day or two is not only helpful, but also a good indicator that even the college's support staff is responsible and informed. Even if you have to call the college's main switchboard to ask where to direct a question, consider it exciting that your teens have questions they want answered! Remember, don't hesitate to add any information you and your teen have learned to your notebook, timeline, or folders. Important details can easily be forgotten if they are not documented. Even if you just put something down on a post-it temporarily and copy it into the appropriate place when you have time, try to keep all the information together. A post-it with X University information on it needs to be attached to the X University folder right when you get the information. If it stays by the computer or the phone, chances are it will end up at the bottom of a pile or be thrown out by mistake, and both your valuable time and information will be lost.

The amount of information you are now gleaning from many sources is helping you to continue your exploration of academic institutions of all sizes, interests, and locations. Even if you and your teens feel the pressure mounting, the constant flow of information at these colleges can prove to be enriching as long as you keep it organized and documented. Reviewing information before your family meetings and updating any new information will be helpful, too, if you can spare the time. The more information you have from each college your teen has an interest in, the easier it will be to make decisions when the time comes.

5
Nuts and Bolts: Get Organized

Organizing is what you do before you do something, so that when you do it, it is not all mixed up.

—A.A. Milne, *Winnie the Pooh*

If I could just get organized, I think I could stay organized, but it's the initial organization that seems so hard for me. My coach gave me some information at practice, and I didn't have anywhere to put it. Things come in the mail, or my guidance counselor gives me some material, and the next thing I know, there's stuff in piles everywhere.

—High school junior

In this chapter we will detail for students the nuts and bolts of the college application process. This information should be used by the teen as a guide and can even serve as a checklist or timeline for students and parents alike. Some parts may not pertain to your particular applications or needs, but pay close attention to each section because each one is important to the application process.

The following pages include a guide to the necessary steps of the college application process. Refer to the material and keep important dates and deadlines in mind. As we said before, make a timeline if you feel it would be helpful. This is particularly useful when either students or parents are struggling to meet deadlines. The timeline gives you a visual overview of the month-to-month expectations for the student and all that he or she needs to accomplish. If a timeline is not for you, try a calendar or a computer checklist that can even alert you when dates are coming due. There are many ways to keep track of these important dates and goals, and it will help tremendously to put at least one technique to work for you during the process, particularly during junior and senior years in high school.

Read through the following information carefully. Feel free to put your own notes in places, but be aware of the possibilities for and advantages of tracking what to do season to season from sophomore year on.

Sophomore Year—Fall:

If your school offers the PSAT in the fall of your sophomore year, sign up for it and take it. It will help get the testing process started at an easy pace, rather than having all the standardized testing occur in junior and senior years. Depending on the score, it may also help determine potential colleges that might be a good fit, and it may encourage you to start thinking about college choices in general.

Sophomore Year—Winter, Spring, Summer:

Stay aware of academic loads and extracurricular interests. Be sure to find a balance between the two. As academic challenges ramp up, organization becomes the key to all facets of your life, even though there is plenty of time for nights out with friends or Sunday afternoon naps that also need to be fit in. This is simply a good time to plant the seeds of future expectations.

If you have any interest in driving by or walking through a college campus nearby, that's a great opportunity to see what awaits the high school grad. If you're vacationing near a college or university, drop in, walk around for a while, and pick up some information to read if the vacation gets boring. This is the year to work your way into the college process and start to get a feel for what college entails. It's simply never too early to explore colleges that are close by or convenient for a trip. Your time spent on campuses is never wasted even if the campus doesn't suit your needs. You can learn something from every place you visit. Comparing and contrasting colleges is valuable and helpful, particularly if you have seen numerous campuses.

There are several test preparation courses to choose from in most areas of the country. Sometimes high schools make them available to students after school or in the evenings, but many classes are given in the testing services' own spaces. Some people recommend private tutoring, which is also a good idea but usually costs more than the general classes. If your learning style points toward individual review, you may want to inquire at the guidance office or through friends who've "been there before" about private tutors. Classes and tutorials can get expensive, and there is not much in the way of financial aid, so decide with your parents what your best approach for test reviewing will be.

Go online to www.collegeboard.com and sign up to receive the SAT Question of the Day or check out www.freerice.com, a vocabulary-building and hunger-ending Web site. At the very least, get some vocabulary flash cards and study one new word each day, taking a few minutes to review all five at the end of each week. It can be part of dinner conversation or something you *do* on your own, but *do* get a start on vocabulary building as a way to stretch your knowledge. Of the students we surveyed, 38 percent said they did review on their own or in class but didn't take any courses. The group that took one or more prep courses or used a tutor totaled 37 percent, but broken down, these percentages change slightly. Public and private university students have different views as do students attending in-state or out-of-state schools (see graph 8). Female students tended to do more reviewing on their own, and all those who said their parents were involved in the process tended to take more review courses—no surprise there!

There are numerous review books for sale at bookstores and through the College Review Board, but there are also practice tests online and in libraries. You may even have access to a review book that an older sibling used, or one that belongs to friend who has just gone off to college. Look into as many possibilities as you can to find the best type of review for your time and budget. It is unproven just how helpful the different programs are; many of the companies have guarantees and statistics, but each company puts its own spin on its successes. Interestingly enough, however, 45 percent of the students *we* polled felt that any testing prep they did was either "extremely helpful or very helpful." Just a little higher, 49 percent of the students who felt they visited the right number of colleges, thought testing preparation was helpful (see graphs 7 through 10).

Junior Year—Fall:

Most schools offer the PSAT/NMSQT (Preliminary Scholastic Assessment Test/National Merit Scholarship Qualifying Test) in October of the junior year. Guidance offices will inform students of the time and date. In November or December the ACT (American College Testing Assessment) is given, and many students are now encouraged to take that test as well.

Begin drawing up a preliminary college list if you haven't already, and meet with your guidance counselor to review what you have chosen for schools. Counselors will probably have other suggestions to add to the lists, and they may be colleges that you haven't thought of. It's so important to always remember that there are many schools that would be a great fit for each student.

If you're a scholarship candidate, start to look into scholarship programs. Home towns, states, and the federal government all have programs, whether one-time grants, continuing grants, scholarships, or loans. Students who start looking for help early can examine numerous possibilities for finding the financial aid they need. Different colleges provide different financial aid packages and amounts of money, but if you as a family have explored all your options, you may be able to pick up some grants or loans to augment the packages colleges offer. There are many, relatively obscure scholarship opportunities to be found online or in guidance offices that frequently go unused simply because students and parents are unaware of them.

Junior Year—Winter:

Be sure to concentrate on academic work. The junior year is well known as one that college admissions offices study. You may be juggling extracurricular activities with academics, but this year's grades are very important.

It's also time to look up dates for SATs (Scholastic Assessment Test) that are offered throughout the year. You can look online or at hard copies in your guidance office for dates, locations, and times. There are deadlines for registration, and some locations fill up quickly, especially in urban areas, so stay on top of the registration and testing dates.

Junior Year—Spring:

Registration for SATs and ACTs (if you are taking them again) should be complete. Individual SAT Achievement tests for specific subjects should be taken in June, when the course work is basically done, and the information is still fresh in your mind. Don't forget, however: you need to register ahead of time.

Look at your college list and see if you can plan some visits for your spring vacation. If you have a few potential colleges near each other, structure your visits so that you can maximize your time. If you have to skip an information session or a tour in one place or another, jot down questions you have and check to see if they can be answered with an online tour at home.

Another tip at this point: start looking for summer work. The early bird gets the worm in this job market, and it's a great time to check places or companies in which you are interested. Saving money for college cannot begin too soon. Just ask your parents!

Before Senior Year—Summer:

Unless they are simply too far away, be sure to visit any colleges on your list that you haven't seen yet. Even though many colleges are officially closed, most run camps or summer programs or actually stay open all year round, so even visiting campuses in the summer gives a surprisingly accurate reading of the school. Tours, information sessions, and admissions offices are open year round, so information is easy to glean.

Try to get applications for all the schools to which you would like to apply. Even if you are planning to use the Common Application, most colleges have their own supplementary essays or requests, and summer is an ideal time to look over each application and learn its requirements. Starting to write the essays now is ideal, especially if you are involved in numerous extracurricular activities. It's often hard to think about starting essays before September, but it avoids incredible tension later in the school year.

College essays basically serve as the heart of each application. Most applications have a number of suggested topics that can be used, and almost all include the possibility of candidates choosing their own essay topics. Regardless of what topic you choose, you must remember that this is your chance to show admissions personnel who you are and why you would be a great addition to their college community. Writing an essay about the amazing accomplishments of a parent or grandparent won't help an admissions officer learn anything new about *you*, the applicant. On the other hand, explaining how you felt about helping a group of special needs children learn how to ride and care for horses could reveal extremely important information about you as a person.

Try to keep a small notebook or its equivalent in a handy place so that if a good essay topic comes to mind, you can jot it down. Too often we think of something important only to forget it later if it's not written down somewhere. If you keep a running list of topics, you may have some great ideas to draw from when it's time to begin writing.

It's difficult to know how much help your parents can be in writing your college essay. Certainly discussing topics and brainstorming can be very helpful for students and parents alike. Work with your parent to select a topic that demonstrates your passion for something specific. It's important, however, for you to focus on the task at hand and your parents ultimately to take a step back. You need to own your own work and will feel your successes only if you *do* own it. The subjects are up for discussion, but the writing needs to be the students'.

A parent's role can frequently be more effective if you share the essay and your parent gives pointers, general suggestions, and even proofreading tips. One parent told us that she suggested her son work on his essay with the parent's close friend, whom the teen regarded highly. This way the parent wasn't overly involved, and the student appreciated the time and suggestions the friend offered up. College counselors, teachers, coaches, and mentors can help advise you as well, but always keep in mind the importance of doing the actual writing and organizational work yourself.

You may feel like you don't want to share your essay with anyone. If this happens, remember the importance of the essay in helping colleges connect with their applicants. Admissions counselors also learn about applicants through teacher recommendations, grades, test scores, and extracurricular activities, but we cannot emphasize strongly enough the importance of essays, which reveal in one way or another the applicant's strengths, interests, struggles, fears, and individuality. Some general suggestions for topics are listed below. Remember, however, you probably have some better ideas of your own!

1. A volunteer job that you felt made a difference
2. A change of attitude because of an experience (positive *or* negative)
3. Relationship with a grandparent, sibling, coach, teacher, neighbor, or mentor that helped you in some way
4. Overcoming a fear of someone or something

Senior Year—Fall:

If you want to take any additional standardized tests, be sure to register for them as quickly as possible so that the scores will arrive in time for the due dates of the colleges to which you are applying. After checking all the applications and determining what you need for recommendations, ask your teachers if they are willing to write you a recommendation. If they are able to, be sure to give them whatever they need (including a stamped envelope addressed to the necessary college). It is also imperative that you ask for recommendations as early as possible, regardless of how you are applying. Too many students ask teachers for help so close to the college application deadlines that it's extremely hard for them to find the time to write the best one possible. They have busy lives, too, and the more time they have to devote to recommendations, the more thoughtful those recommendations will be.

Check in regularly with your guidance counselor. You have notebooks and deadlines with information at home, but you may want to be sure the guidance department has all the information you have, and that your application deadlines concur. The guidance office must send out transcripts and numerous forms colleges require, so don't hesitate to check and make sure that the right forms have gone to the right schools in a timely fashion.

The last part of this section is that you, the student, need to fill out the applications to the college (if you're applying early) or colleges as soon as you can. Certainly, if you're applying early with a November deadline, be sure to have everything done as close to October 1 as possible. Other applications, which can be due any time from December to March, can wait a little longer, but it's not wise to leave submissions until the deadline. College admissions officers appreciate receiving applications well before the deadline so that they can process the folders and get organized themselves. You are welcome at any time to send an incomplete application; this will help the college get your folder started. Just be sure you let them know what else will be coming.

Senior Year—Winter:

If you haven't finished your applications, ***do them now!*** Even if you are applying online and not depending on the mail service, we can't emphasize enough the value of getting your applications done ahead of deadlines. Put off the movies, scratch the video games. Get those applications in ***now!***

We also *highly* recommend that you make a hard copy, a duplicate of every application you send, whether it goes through online or regular mail. You can place a backup of each application in your file or notebook and college folder, where it can be found easily if necessary. It will serve as proof of the times and dates you have submitted the forms and will help you if you need to refer to the application for any reason. Applications *can* get lost in the mail or misplaced in an admissions office, so it is in your best interest to protect your applications with duplicates that include dates.

If you need financial aid, it's time to fill out the FAFSA (Free Application for Federal Student Aid) forms, which you can get in your guidance office or download from the Internet. You will need a number of family forms like W-2s, tax forms, bank statements, and your own proof of identity, such as a license or passport. Both students and parents will need Personal Identification Numbers (PINs) which you can establish at the www.pin.ed.gov Web site. The forms should be mailed by January 1, and you will receive the results of your application in about a month. It is called the SAR (Student Aid Report), and you need to double-check the information contained in it. If there are errors on the SAR, make the corrections on the form that is provided and return it to the address you are given. Once any necessary corrections have been made, you also want to make sure that all the colleges you applied to have copies of your report.

Some colleges also require you to fill out a CSS Profile for scholarships from private sources within specific colleges. This is a wonderful way to add to your financial aid package since most private funding is in the form of gifts, not loans. Almost all colleges are "need blind" now, meaning they do not consider your financial needs when looking at your application for admission. It's imperative, however, that the admissions office knows what your needs are so they can try to meet them if they admit you as a student. Each college has a "pie" from which to draw its financial aid, some larger than others, and if you need a piece of that pie, be sure your forms are in order.

There are many helpful Web sites that explain the complexities of financial aid. Some of the best and most user-friendly are: www.fastweb.com, www.finaid.org, www.fafsa.com, www.mefa.org/index.php, and www.collegeboard.com/article/0,,6-29-0-401,00.html. If you still have questions after checking Web sites and your forms, try contacting your guidance office. Many guidance counselors have had a great deal of experience with financial aid, and they should be able to help you.

Senior Year—Spring:

You will begin receiving acceptances, deferrals , and rejections by mid-March if you have applied "regular" decision . As we said in chapter 7, take time to make your decisions and visit or revisit the schools to which you have been accepted. Usually you can take until May 1 to make up your mind, so talk to counselors, teachers, coaches, mentors, parents, and friends before you make any hasty decisions.

If you are looking for the best combination of financial package and college, don't hesitate to talk to the financial aid offices at your favorite schools. Grants, loans, and work hours are usually set, but there may be some other resources (like small banks with low-interest student loans) that financial aid officers will recommend. You may have to be a little creative financially, but you will feel it's worth it.

Extra Material::

If you are planning on making tapes or CDs to serve as résumés highlighting academic, music, drama, club, or athletic specialties, try to establish a well-organized plan to showcase your talent. Professional photographers and recording coaches can be extremely expensive and hard to book, especially if students are away at boarding schools. If you have the means to make tapes and CDs, research and employ help as early as possible. Lacrosse players, for example, need to be filmed during the spring of their junior year; senior year is simply too late. A musician may need to reserve a heavily scheduled practice room, so don't wait until the last minute to prepare special items.

It's also wise for coaches and professionals to receive your materials well ahead of your visit so that they can be well informed of your specific talents. If you're a soccer goalie and the team already has two or three goalies, the coach may not be very interested in your skills. If you're a French horn player and the conductor just graduated his first chair French horn player, then be sure to sell yourself as an eager musician. The quality of your work is extremely important, but your own personality will come through as well, and hopefully it will create a winning combination. We must be honest, here, however, that many students are eager to continue their specialties into their college years, and they are often disappointed because their experience doesn't meet the college's expectations. It's important to remember that college athletes are *all good at what they do; that's why they're continuing to play their sport. Extracurricular activities are more specialized in college as a way for students to grow in their sport or special interest...*

Students interested in theater and music may be able to find help online to augment their talents. In Massachusetts, for example, the Massachusetts High School Drama Guild has a Web site: www.mhsdg.com/index.html. Music departments in Massachusetts often steer their students to http://menc.org/networks/collegiate/NailThatAudition.html. Because theater and music students frequently have to perform for colleges or send tapes similar to the tapes athletes send, it's important to plan well ahead for whatever interest the student is planning to promote.

A final reminder: extracurricular activities may simply not work out, as the time they take may interfere with academics or other interests. Division I schools in particular expect a full-time commitment from their students and frequently house them in separate dorms complete with dining halls and study facilities. You may find your social life centered on your extracurricular activities, but take care to keep your college life academically oriented and enriching if possible. It can often be seductive to pursue things besides academics at college, and it's far too easy to fall behind academically if you aren't careful. Organization is an important cornerstone of college life, and priorities must be set early if you are to reach your full potential at any institution.

6
Decisions, Decisions: Learn All You Can

I had the story bit by bit, from various people, and as generally happens in such cases, each time it was a different story.

—Edith Wharton, *Ethan Frome*

I felt like I'd been waiting forever to hear from colleges, but once I really heard that I was accepted to more than one, I wasn't quite sure how to decide which one!

—College student

Once April rolls around and rejections, deferrals, and acceptances are received, the pressure on both student and parents seems to lessen. Even if there are disappointments, the reality of decision making is at hand, and the process of finding a good college fit is now in *your* hands. Campuses hold visiting days. You can visit or revisit a campus to find out more information. You can e-mail or call the contacts you have made at the various campuses you are considering. If you have not made any contacts with certain schools other than submitting an application, then *learn all you can*. Try to connect with students, professors, coaches, or other personnel. There are reasons these colleges have accepted you. Find out what is appealing and important about those schools. If you are the student in the household, *you* are in charge of the decisions at this point, so you need to arm yourself with as much knowledge as you can to make the most informed decisions you can. It's exciting to go to college. It widens horizons and changes lives in ways no one will know ahead of time, so embrace this part and enjoy the process.

Start by organizing as many visits as a family, even return visits, as possible, especially if an Accepted Student Visiting Day fits into your schedule and budget. The energy on campus during these days is very indicative of the effort colleges put forth to entice students to choose them. By attending a class or panel discussion, having lunch with a coach, mentor, or professor, and even touring parts of the campus for the first time or a return trip, students and parents should gain valuable input to help make the final decision about which college to attend. Even on these visits, be sure to take your college notebook or folders and continue to jot down important information. If you are visiting more than one school, be sure not to confuse information, and update your files as quickly as possible (on the plane ride, train, bus, or car ride returning home would be ideal!), so that details will stay fresh and unencumbered.

At this point, you may also know more about what you are looking for in colleges where you have been accepted. It can easily be a year since you have seen the campuses to which you have been accepted, and new academic interests may have arisen during that time. Your extracurricular or athletic interests may have also developed or changed, and a little extra research concerning new or developed areas of interest before visiting or revisiting a college could prove extremely helpful. The key is finding the most pertinent parts of the College Visiting Days and making use of them. Even though prearranged days can be a bit of a show-and-tell time, they are always informative and helpful in the decision-making process—even if the visit helps you to cross a college *off* your list.

If you haven't already, acquire as many course catalogs as you can, remembering that many of them are online now. *Study* the general course offerings such as arts and sciences and specific departments, for example biology and calculus if you already have some particular interests. Psychology and sociology departments often differ in their requirements, how they list courses, how they offer lab and research courses, and how they conduct seminars. Science and math departments frequently have courses for nonmajors so that requirements can be fulfilled. Check on these possibilities. History, foreign languages, and English courses can often be easier to interpret than some departments, but in all cases, pay attention to upper-level courses and requirements. There may be ways to combine majors and departments that interest you. Check the possibilities out. Don't forget to consider how a major or department of interest might carry you to a semester or year abroad or even to a different institution in the United States for a semester. Students are taking semesters away from their colleges at an ever increasing rate, and you should look into what the various colleges you are considering can offer along these lines and what their requirements are. Some programs are definitely more rigorous than others, but in general, the amount of work the student puts in corresponds directly with the value of the completed semester. Frequently, colleges work together with study-abroad programs to accommodate students, but you would want to know details ahead of time if at all possible.

Another way to evaluate colleges you have been accepted to is to return to Web sites and recheck what interests you. Departments, whether their fields are academics, sports, or general extracurricular activities, should all be user-friendly and relatively easy to find. If for some reason the information is hard to locate, consider two things: is the department well organized and ready for you, and is the college up to date with important information and technology? Students and parents should be able to find answers to any of their questions with relative ease, and should note any necessary details, positive or negative, regarding online research campus-wide. A simple question like the number of students currently attending a given school may be right on the front page of a college's online brochure, with a little-known fact regarding a science professor's latest book being much more difficult to find. Each piece of information, however, should be available even if somewhat hidden. Today College Web Sites can be excellent indicators of the college's ability and willingness to embrace technology in all parts of its system.

Another technique for finding out answers to important questions is growing in use and popularity: many campuses now sponsor evenings when high school students can e-mail or call numbers where college students are ready to answer questions. These evenings are spaced throughout the academic calendar and include times before and after college admissions. Computer and phone centers are set up for several hours at a time and have been increasingly well utilized by high school students. Many times, high school students may have questions that they are not comfortable asking in large groups, with their parents in tow, or face to face, so the e-mail and phone call times create opportunities not found by other means. The high school students may even find a comfort level with a particular college student that could extend past established calling or computer hours and become helpful for future reference.

If you know students at a school you have been accepted to, you also have the opportunity to visit them. This idea has its pros and cons simply because of scheduling, different interests, and expectations. It can certainly be fun for high school students to spend time with college kids on campuses. Our own experiences, however, and those of many other parents, lead us to believe this is not a way to *maximize* learning all that many colleges have to offer. It should, perhaps, be seen as an *additional* way to view a school and its campus life, and get a handle on the student population and dorm life.

You may also reflect on the process that has been part of your life for the last several years. Many of our friends, and in fact, many of the students we polled, had a number of ideas they offered up to help future students and parents. Although we have incorporated these ideas into the book in various places, it's important to list a few things here as well. So many students felt that parental support was invaluable even if they did not communicate that during the process. We were surprised that students in general did not seek or feel support from many of their friends. Many of them felt competition with their friends, although those feelings rarely played themselves out in interactions among the teens. Instead, they basically avoided talking about college with their friends, worried that they would hurt a friend's feelings or appear conceited or unconcerned. There is an exaggerated sense of success and failure now among many high school students regarding both their academics and extracurricular activities, and the college decision process can often be an extension of the pressures of high school. We found that most students just wanted to avoid the whole college topic as much as possible with their friends. They knew that guidance counselors, teachers, mentors, and parents would give them ample time to think about and work on college material. Many of them did admit that they would have liked to share more with their peers, but again, most of them said that the positives and negatives of the college selection process were simply too intense to discuss.

Similarly, parents often felt a sense of competition with other parents. In retrospect, they wished that the competitive parts of the college process had not been so pronounced. Too frequently, parents admitted, they connected their own sense of self-worth with the college choices their sons and daughters were making. They were quick to point out that their own concerns sometimes took precedence over those of their children, and in hindsight they wished they had been able to control their own doubts and worries better. Parents of students who had already been through the process felt they could be more honest with other parents, but even then, whether their teen was the first child or the last in their household, each experience was different, and the pressures were always there in one form or another.

One of the main reasons behind writing this book was our realization that each child and each college experience is surprisingly different. Sharing your knowledge with other parents is invaluable, but what works for one student may be a total failure for another. Each parent and each student needs to remember what works for each individual. There may be similarities in siblings, and one brother or sister may be eager to follow in an older sibling's footsteps, but don't be discouraged if your younger children want to strike out on their own and make their own path. Many brothers and sisters find the closeness they can maintain at the same school to be reassuring and fun. Periodic dinners together and rides to and from home can be wonderful times to connect. Colleges, even small ones, tend to have populations of well over a thousand, so it is unlikely siblings would be constantly running into each other, but as parents we need to remember that each teen has a different need for independence, and attending the same college may not be something certain brothers and sisters want to do. There are advantages and disadvantages for parents and siblings alike to apply to the same college or even a parent's alma mater, but it is most important that your teen feels free to make those kinds of decisions with no feelings of guilt or obligation.

7
The End Is Really Only a New Beginning

All this happened, more or less.
       —Kurt Vonnegut, *Slaughterhouse Five*

I see far too many kids getting caught up on names… whatever the "flavor of the month" is. Then for many it's almost as if nothing else "counts" (I even ran into this personally 25 years ago—got into Cornell and Tufts but chose Northeastern and met with a lot of puzzled looks). It's so important for kids to know themselves, and what their interests and passions are— not necessarily what they "want to be." Many kids have just followed the prescribed school routines and get to senior year without really knowing what they're into … They truly have to listen to themselves—something they're not always used to doing. We breed kids that are eager to please and succeed, and too often they've learned that one of the best ways to do this is to listen to others' opinions above their own.
       —Middle school teacher and high school coach

Although we invite you all as parents, grandparents, aunts, uncles, legal guardians, and siblings, to read this chapter, it is actually devoted to the students: the seniors in high school who have just been accepted to college. We will direct our advice specifically to them and hope that it will help them as they decide what their final college choice will be.

First of all, congratulations! Not only have you completed a very long and exhaustive process, but you have been rewarded by acceptance to college! The most challenging part of the process is behind you, although you may also be finding it difficult to make the final decision of which college you would most like to attend. We'll try to include all the possible combinations of decision making, so feel free to skim parts that do not apply to your specific needs.

To start with, if you applied early decision to a college and were accepted, then you have made a commitment to that college, and you are on your way. Fast forward through the next few pages, past all the various college acceptance variations. Don't forget, however, that you are invited to the college's Accepted Student Days, and visiting the school again and connecting with various departments might be a great way to reconnect and add excitement to your decision.

If you have been accepted to one college, and you feel you would like to attend it, then once again, you are on your way. If you are feeling unsure about the college that has accepted you, then take this opportunity to learn all over again just why you applied. If you have already visited the college, and it is too far away to revisit, then don't hesitate to go online and take another virtual tour, checking out academic departments and extracurricular activities. E-mail professors and feel free to call the admissions office. Admissions personnel may be able to answer any questions you have or direct your questions to other people or departments. You have a wonderful opportunity to learn about this school and begin to make it your own. You may even be able to e-mail students on campus, many of whom volunteer to talk to prospective students online and answer any questions you might have.

It is ideal, however, if you can revisit the school. As mentioned earlier, most schools have days when they invite accepted students back to campus. On those days, there are special events and information sessions for both students *and* parents, and they are hosted by administrators, professors, coaches, and students. If you have already made contacts with coaches, professors, or financial aid personnel, make an appointment ahead of time to meet with them again for help with any outstanding issues you may still have. Walk the campus again and visit any areas of study you may be interested in. Explore the course of studies catalog and pay attention to its many offerings. Go to a cafeteria or student union and strike up a conversation with a student.

In our travels to numerous campuses, we found that most students are eager to talk about their college experiences, whether positive or negative. Discussions with students, even in the online sessions that some colleges provide, reveal a great deal about campus life and the pulse of its student population. Our research with college students showed that the number of colleges they were accepted to was less important than the knowledge they gained from their research into each college. They were eager to attend the one college they were accepted to if they had seen at least several other schools. They were less satisfied if they hadn't seen numerous campuses. A surprising 56 percent of those applicants who applied to between two and five colleges said that they wished they had visited more colleges before applying. Of those who visited between six and ten colleges, 15 percent wished they had seen more while almost 33 percent of those who visited six or more colleges felt they had seen the "right" number (see graphs 11 and 12). Be the detective at this point. Try to ferret out answers to any remaining questions you may have; doing so will give you confidence that you are making the right decision. Interestingly enough, despite all the extras that students and parents are looking for at various colleges, over 91 percent of the college students we polled rated "the quality of education" as the most important criterion for their decision in choosing the college they were attending (see graphs 13 through 16).

Now let's consider some more options. If you have been accepted to more than one college, don't hesitate to take some time to make your decision. Most colleges inform their prospective students by late March or early April but do not require a commitment from students applying for regular admission until the May 1. Feel free at this point to explore all the possibilities each college will offer *you*. Return to the college that accepted you on early action . Even though you did not have to commit to them early, they committed to you. What does that say about their faith in you? It's clear they want you to attend their school. Be sure to give them as much time as the other schools that accepted you. Just because you heard from them before the others doesn't make them less important.

Many colleges have also started offering merit scholarships, grants, and paid internships as a way to entice applicants. These opportunities can give you a jump start on your college experience, and should be considered important for both students and parents alike. Be sure to take advantage of visiting days offered to accepted students. Each college hopes you will attend its school, and lectures, question-and-answer periods, workshops, extracurricular events, and visits to classes are all scheduled into the visiting day, giving you the opportunity to make some important comparisons among the schools you are considering. Be sure to make appointments with professors, deans, or coaches if you have questions concerning how *you* will truly fit into the programs that are important to you at each campus. You certainly may change your focus as you grow through your college years, but take advantage of what interests you have at this point in your life and make sure that the college you choose will complement those interests.

We also recommend that you take a notebook to your college visits and write down anything that comes to mind. You may even want your parents to do the same, since you may be in separate workshops and can compare impressions after the visits. The notebook will be helpful for rating what is important to you on each campus: for example, a certain academic or athletic department, dorm life, possible off-campus housing, financial aid, and the school's location relative to cities as well as to home. Try to immerse yourself as much as possible in the culture of the college each time. That will help you figure out which school best fits your needs and interests.

Waiting lists for students make deciding on college choices more difficult. Very frequently, if you are wait-listed, you will not hear from that school one way or the other before the May 1 deadline. At this point, consider the options before you. If you are wait-listed at a school you are not really interested in attending, then drop that school from your list of possible choices. Let them know (they usually include a postcard offering you the choice to stay on the waiting list or decline the position). This way you will open up the list for students who are truly interested in the school and will attend if given the choice.

Many schools, however, do not take students off their waiting lists at all depending on the admissions pool, and the ones that do may make you wait for several months as they garner their own student population. If you are certain you want to attend the school that has put you on its waiting list, here are some strategies to help you gain admittance. First of all, write a letter right away to the dean of admissions stating that you understand the decision, but you would still like to attend the school. The letter should be short but can include whatever reasons you think the school would benefit from having a student like you on that campus. There is an example of a waiting list letter included in the last chapter. At the same time, make an appointment with your guidance counselor and see what the two of you can do together to reinforce your viability as a student. Guidance counselors are informed of college decisions at the same time as students, so they should be ready to step forward in your support at this time. Any new information, such as academic honors, extracurricular achievements, or community service awards you've won since you submitted your application, can be forwarded to the college where you are wait-listed. The admissions office keeps all these files open, so your added information may give you an edge over the students who are simply "waiting to see what happens." Don't be afraid to be an advocate for yourself at this point. Admissions professionals *want* to hear why you still wish to attend their school. If you are wait-listed, it's not because you are unqualified. More often than not, a wait-listed student has excellent qualifications for the desired school. It may simply be a question of space, so keep trying to convince the personnel that you will make great use of their space if they provide it for you.

If you do not receive an acceptance that you have been taken off a waiting list before the regular May 1 deadline, commit to your second college choice. Here again, you can make a decision to let the wait-listed college go or continue waiting. If you are going to continue to wait, we suggest that you and your guidance counselor send another letter reinforcing your wish to attend the school. If you are willing to wait through the summer, make that clear as well. One never knows what may arise on a campus over the summer that will open up student spaces. A final option you can try is to inform the school that you are willing to wait until the following calendar year to start college if they will guarantee you a spot. While waiting a year may seem difficult, there are many other opportunities for the high school graduate, and a year of working mixed with some well-planned activities can be an incredible opportunity to grow. One student we know received admission to the college of his choice for the year after his high school graduation, and he took the opportunity to coach a football team, work at a restaurant, make a folk guitar, and spend the summer working in the national parks system. By the time he went to college, he had enriched his life tremendously and felt much more mature and self-confident, readier than many of his former high school buddies to meet the college challenge.

The obvious disadvantage to staying on a waiting list is that you don't have the opportunity to bond with a school at the same time as most other students. If you are feeling caught between two spaces, our advice is to embrace the college you have accepted and keep the wait-list school on your radar but not front and center. Professionals as well as parents are hoping that college applicants will enjoy a sense of success and satisfaction once they have been through the college application process, so it is in your best interest to celebrate your accomplishments and acceptances and look toward the future. Your flexibility in both your college decision and your ability to wait for another college to accept you will teach you to value the school you attend even more.

Whether you were accepted early decision or waited to decide until the last minute, once you decide on a certain college, don't look back! You've made a great decision based on your choices and all the hard work you have done to date. You've gotten to know the school where you are going to hang your hat for the next few years. Buy a T-shirt or sweatshirt and a sticker for the family car. That way you won't need to answer the constant question you used to hear: "Where do you want to go to college?" After May 1, everyone will be asking "Where *are* you going to college?" By wearing something with your college's logo on it, you answer the question before it gets asked. Now the only problem is that the same nosy person who wanted answers to those two questions will now ask you what you want to major in—we can't help you with that just now! Our advice is: celebrate, celebrate! You have finished the college application and admission process. Now you can look forward to beginning a new chapter in your life, full of new experiences, both enriching and challenging. Again, you have our heartiest congratulations!

8

How Resourceful Are We?

Ships at a distance have every man's wisdom on board.
—Zora Neale Hurston, Their Eyes Were Watching God

What surprised me was how hard it was to stay organized. I had all my responsibilities as a senior in high school, and then I had all this extra work to look at colleges and prepare applications. Staying on top of college deadlines and my own work was much harder than I thought. I know now that I'm going to make my little brother plan ahead and stay organized!

—High school senior

This chapter is actually a workbook for students and their families. We have included the formats and information we used, and we have also included some ideas we *wish* in retrospect that we *had* used! Feel free to copy any of the information in this chapter and use it in your notebooks, correspondences, and files. Or better yet, use the information provided here and make it your own. We start with a page we call "The College Application Worksheet" and follow it with checklists, résumés, and sample letters. The reason we feel this book will help students and parents alike is that we shared so many ideas with each other, professionals, college students, and parents who are going through the same college-related issues. Be sure to incorporate anything you can from the colleges you research in addition to what is provided here. Each year colleges may reformat applications, e-mails, or phone numbers, and coaches and academic departments may change with little or no warning. Don't assume that all things about a school remain the same year after year.

Check the charts graphs from the student questionnaires we administered. They describe the college application from the students' points of view. Some results are surprising, some almost too obvious. All are helpful in your application process in some way or another.

Remember—get the most out of your family meetings. Parents, try to stay open to all communication with your teen and with the schools he or she is interested in. Stay as organized as you can during this journey by using any tools offered in this book and by using your own ideas as well. Be positive with each other, guidance counselors, teachers, college professionals, and friends. As much as this whole process often has an incredibly competitive feel to it, it's not really about the competition at all. The college search is honestly about finding a place where students would like to further their education, expand their experiences, and grow personally and professionally. There is not just one school for anyone. So many schools, particularly now, have so very much to offer. With added communication, good organization, and hard work, you can each make this process more rewarding. Don't hesitate to advise your friends and family once you look back on all that you have accomplished. Wouldn't it feel great to alleviate some of the stress *you* felt to make a friend's college search easier—hey, even brothers and sisters can use a little advice from their older siblings now and then! We look forward to hearing your feedback!

College Application Worksheet

College	Application deadline	Fee	Testing requirements	Interview	**Additional requirements**
College A 50 Main St. Anywhere, USA	Jan 1 (regular) Nov 1 Early action (nonbinding)	$65	SAT I or ACT and 3 SAT II subject tests	Alumni if possible	Two teachers' recommendation Common Application + "College A" Supplement
College B 25 School Street Booksville, USA	Jan 1 (regular) Nov 1 ED (binding)	$70	SAT I or ACT and 2 SAT II subject tests	Optional but will be considered— On-campus (only to rising seniors) or alumni	Two teachers' recommendation Common Application + "College B" pre-application + peer evaluation
College C 10 Elm St. Collegetown, USA	Feb 1 (regular) Dec 1 Early action (nonbinding)	$60	SAT I or ACT optional	Strongly recommended	Two teachers' recommendation Common Application
College D 35 Oak St. Dreamtown, USA	March 15 (regular) Rolling and early notification within two weeks of applying	$30 (waived if submitted online)	SAT I or ACT optional	Optional	Two teachers' recommendation Common Application Optional— additional essay and photo
College E 100 Great Rd. Easton, USA	Jan 15 (regular) Nov 1 Early action (nonbinding)	$50	SAT I or ACT required	Required	One teacher's recommendation Common Application
College F 75 Pleasant St. Factville, USA	Feb 15 (regular)	$50— Waived if visit to campus before applying	Optional	Optional	Two teachers' recommendation Common Application

College Form Checklist

College name and location: _____

Travel method, travel time: _____

_____

Student population: _____

_____

Any personal contacts: (professors, coaches, students—include phone number and e-mail)

_____

Strengths: _____

_____

Weaknesses: _____

_____

Immediate student feedback: _____

_____

_____

Immediate parent feedback: _____

_____

_____

Ten-day revisit feedback (don't look at previous notes): _____

_____

Was there anything about this visit that worked particularly well or poorly, and why?

_____

Student Athletic Résumé

Each athlete will have to construct his or her individual résumé. If you participate in a timed sport like swimming, skiing, or track, line your events up on the left and list your times by the calendar year:

	2005	2006	2007	2008
100-yard free	52.4	51.2	50.0	49.7

List any and all of your events in a similar fashion. That way coaches can see your progress and know whether you could be an asset to their particular team. This is also a good time to list any special meets or events you and/or your team participated in each year.

Sports like wrestling, fencing, karate, and volleyball have team totals as well as individual totals, but also keep track of other parts of the scores, like pins and kills. Be sure to complete your scoring regarding your sport, as the more information your coach can gain, the more helpful it will be for him or her. Help your coach decide why you should be on the team!

Sports like field hockey, ice hockey, soccer, football, baseball, softball, and lacrosse may be a little harder when it comes to finding ways to showcase your skills. For example, even though goal totals and rebounds are recorded, it may be harder to show yourself as a "standout." Find ways to point out your strengths, and be sure your high school coach can help communicate your strengths as a player and a teammate with an athletic résumé. Two examples of athletic résumés follow, or you can always feel free to find examples on "athletic résumé" Web sites.

ATHLETICS SUMMARY RÉSUMÉ

NAME: Polly Pocket
ADDRESS: 31 Maple Street
              Any Town, MA 02202

GRADUATION: June 2008
G.P.A.: N/A
HONOR ROLL: 2005 (4 of 4)
2006 (4 of 4)
2007 (3 of 4)

TELEPHONE:
E-MAIL:
HEIGHT: WEIGHT:
HIGH SCHOOL ATHLETICS:
FIELD HOCKEY: VARSITY 2004, 2005, 2006, 2007
                 Position: Left Midfield, Center Midfield
                 Dual County League Champions 2005, 2006, 2007
                 North Sectional Champions 2005, 2006, 2007
                 Eastern Mass Champions: 2006, 2007
                 Cape Ann Club Hockey: 2006 Field Hockey Festival,
                 Indio, California,
                 Futures: 2002-2007

BASKETBALL: VARSITY 2004–05, 2005–06, 2006–07, 2007–08
Position: Guard, Point Guard; 650+ points scored to date
Junior National Basketball Massachusetts Team, Columbus, Ohio: 2006, 2007

LACROSSE: VARSITY 2005, 2006, 2007, 2008

Position: Third Home, Second Home, Center, Left Attack Wing
Bay State Games, North Team: 2007, 2008
Team Revolution: Club Team with Nation Lacrosse—Spring 2008

ATHLETIC HONORS:

Dual County League All Star: Basketball: 2006, 2007, 2008
                                      Lacrosse: 2006, 2007, 2008
                                      Field Hockey: 2006, 2007
Anytown High School Scholar Athlete: 2006, 2007, 2008
Metro West Basketball All Star: 2007, 2008

Student Name: Hope Tobe

Profile:

Class:	Position:
Senior	Center Midfield
Hometown:	Birthdate:
Anytown, Ma.	4/25/91
High School:	
Anytown High	

Field Hockey Background:

Two years USFHA Futures Participant
Cape Ann Coalition member 2001–2008
USFHA National Field Hockey Festival participant 2006
USFHA National Field Hockey Festival participant 2007
Anytown High School Varsity team member 2004-2007
Helped lead High School Field Hockey Team to Eastern States Final as a freshman—2005
Helped lead High School Field Hockey Team to Division I State Final as a sophomore—2006
Helped lead High School Field Hockey Team to Division I State Final as a junior—2007
Helped lead High School Field Hockey Team to Dual County League Championships—2005, 2006, 2007

Athletic Background:

Varsity Field Hockey Team member (midfield) 2004, 2005, 2006, 2007 (Co-Captain 2007)
Varsity Lacrosse Team member (center, third home) 2005, 2006, 2007, 2008
Varsity Basketball Team member (guard) 2005, 2006, 2007, 2008
Dual County League All Star: Field Hockey 2007, Lacrosse 2006, 2007, 2008 Basketball 2006, 2007, 2008
Metro West All Star: Basketball 2008, Field Hockey 2007
Best of Sixty All Star Field Hockey Team 2007

Boston Herald All Scholastic Field Hockey Team 2007

Academics:

Honor Roll Student: 2004–2008
GPA: 3.43
Anytown High School Scholar Athlete 2006, 2007, 2008

Extracurricular:

Class Secretary: 2005, 2006, 2007
Class Vice President: 2007–08
Anytown Interact Community Service Club: 2007 to present
Anytown International Affiliation: 2006 to present
Coach—"Little Chix with Stix" (youth field hockey program) 2005 to present
Coach: CYO Basketball U10 girls 2006 to present
Youth Leader: St. Peter's Episcopal Church, Anytown, MA 2004–2008

Personal:

Father: name and interests
Mother: name and interests
Brother: name, Middlebury College 2005, current hobbies: biker, triathlete
Brother: name, Tufts University 2007, current hobbies: music

Anna Stage

| Height: | Hair: | E-mail: |
| Weight: | Eyes: | Phone number: |

Drama

Stephanie*	*Mitosis*	Lead	2004
Angelo's Servant	*Measure for Measure*	Minor	2005
Leila	*Escaping Alcestis*	Supporting	2005
Mama	*Mariner*	Supporting	2006
Sophie*	*Chairs*	Lead	2006
Lucianna**	*A Comedy of Errors*	Supporting	2006
Prudence	*Beyond Therapy*	Lead	2006
Lady Percy	*Henry IV*	Supporting	2006
Sofia	*Uncle Vanya*	Lead	2007
Third Gentleman	*A Winter's Tale*	Featured	2007
Emma Ross*	*The Outlier Effect*	Lead	2007
Matilda	*The Castle of Otranto*	Lead	2007
Countess**	*Mad Woman of Chaillot*	Lead	2007
Smitty**	*Cry Havoc*	Lead	2007
Madame Pinchard	*An Absolute Turkey*	Featured	2007
Samantha Merrill	*Painting Provenance*	Lead	2008

Musical

Officer Barrel	*Urinetown*	Featured	2004
Sally Brown	*You're a Good Man, Charlie Brown*	Lead	2004
Motel's Sister	*Fiddler on the Roof*	Minor	2005
Roberta/Maggie	*Working*	Lead	2005
Donna Marie	*Blood Brothers*	Minor	2006
Aunt Sadie	*My Favorite Year*	Featured	2007

Film

Caroline	Educational Film/ Boston University	Supporting	2007

Training

Voice	Mr. Tom Osterling	3 years (Classical)
Theatre	Mr. John Minigan	4 years
Theatre	Mr. Aidan O'Hara	4 years
Voice	Ms. Valeri Schleppi	2 years (Broadway)

Theatre   Mr. Ryan Lee   1 month
                                       (Sense Memory Technique)

*Denotes an award-winning role, accredited by the _____
association
** Denotes a role that received an award from _____Center for the
Performing Arts

Heather Tune

Height: Hair: Phone Number:
Weight: Eyes: E-mail:

Voice category:

Home address: Street, City, State, Zip
High School:
Street
City, State, Zip

Musical Education: (Include names of voice or instrument teachers, coaches, and conductors, and the length of time spent studying with each)

Languages Studied: (Include years studied and general proficiency—fluent, excellent, good, poor)

Italian: French:

German: Spanish:

Other:

TOEFL (test of English as a foreign language) score:
Date:

Performance experience: (Include dates)

Performance awards: (Include dates)

Enclosed tape includes:

(Theater, Instrumental, and Voice résumés can be a combination of the above résumés.)

Sample Student Letter to Athletic Coach

(Can be formatted for academics and any other extracurricular interest—
keep it short and specific)

Street address
Town and state address
Date

Name of professional
Title
Office address (if appropriate)
Street address
State address

Dear (name of professional),

I am planning a visit to your campus sometime during my April (February, March, specific weekend) school vacation week, which runs from April x to x. I would like to meet with you at your convenience to learn about your _____ program and the possibility of playing in college with your team. I am including my athletic résumé and a CD of several of my games, including games on turf as well as grass.

I will look forward to hearing from you by mail, e-mail, or phone to arrange a specific meeting time. My address is listed above, my e-mail is:_____, and my phone number is: xxx-xxx-xxxx. I am eager to continue playing _____ in college, and I hope you will consider me as a valuable addition to your program. Thank you again for your time.

Sincerely,

(Type full name, phone number, and e-mail here and sign your name above.)

Sample Follow-up/Thank-you Letter
(Can be formatted for any extracurricular or academic interest as well as sports—remember: short and specific)

Street address
Town and state address
Date

Name of professional
Title
Office address (if appropriate)
Street address
State address

Dear (name of professional),

Thank you so much for meeting with me last (day, date, and time). It was great to learn more about your program specifically and the team schedule and responsibilities in general. I was particularly interested in _____ _____. If you have any further questions for me or need any more information, please don't hesitate to contact me. I will look forward to hearing from you, and I will keep you up to date with my season as well. Thanks again.

Sincerely,

(Type full name, phone number
and e-mail here and sign
your name above.)

Sample Follow-Up Waiting List Letter

Street address
Town, state & zip
Date

Name of admissions director
Title
College name
Street address
Town, state & zip

Dear (name of admissions director),

Although I was hoping to be chosen for admission to _____,
thank you for placing me on your waiting list. _____
_____ is still my number-one choice for college, so I would like to stay
on your waiting list. I would also like you to know that after my application
was submitted, I won a National Debate Team Honorable Mention and was
named to the Basketball Dual County League All Stars Team. I made third
term honor roll and will be working hard to keep my grades high. I will also
let you know if any other awards or honors come my way.

Again, I respect your decision, and I will be sure to do my best to make
myself an even better candidate as the school year progresses. I'll look forward to hearing from you. Thank you for your time.

Sincerely,

I.M. Hopeful
(Type full name, phone number
and e-mail here and sign
your name above.)

College Research Graphs

During the fall of 2005 and the winter of 2006, we visited seven colleges across the country: Lewis & Clark College (OR), Miami University (OH), Middlebury College (VT), Ohio State University (OH), Ohio Wesleyan University (OH), Regis College (MA), Tufts University (MA), The University of Oregon at Eugene (OR), Wheaton College (MA), and Willamette University (OR). We surveyed over fifteen hundred college students. The following bar graphs present the data collected from the survey.

#1 When did you Start the College Process?
Before Junior Year Summary

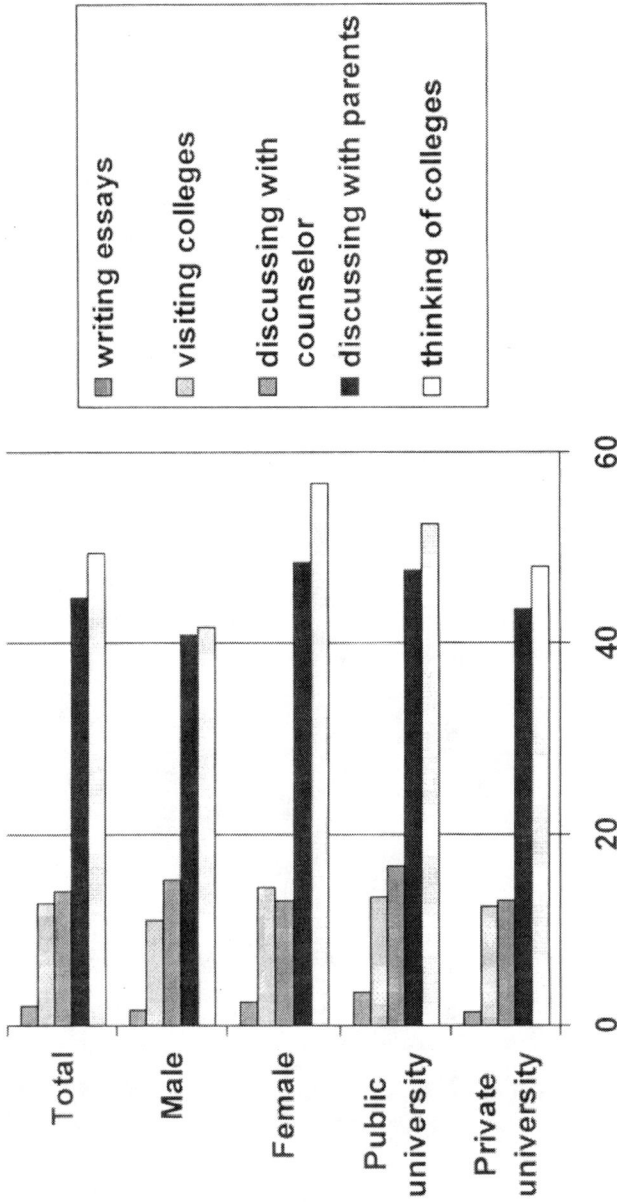

Legend:
- writing essays
- visiting colleges
- discussing with counselor
- discussing with parents
- thinking of colleges

Categories: Total, Male, Female, Public university, Private university

Callow Nichols Research Stucy   Table 1 - 6

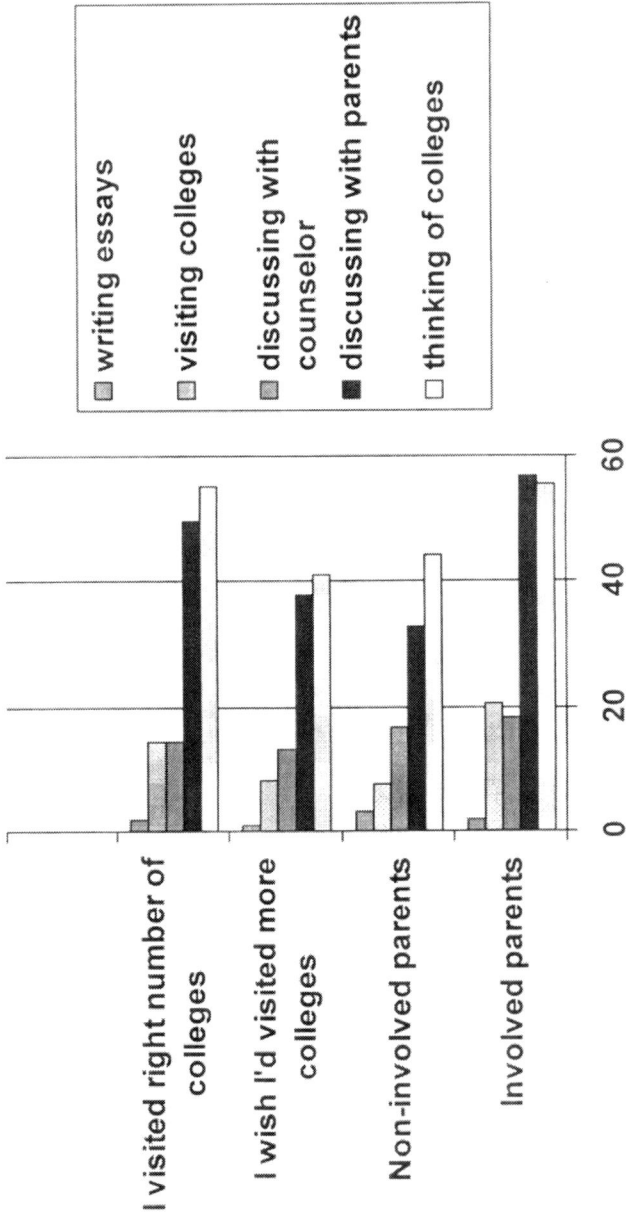

#2 When did you Start the College Process?
Before Junior Year Summary

Legend:
- writing essays
- visiting colleges
- discussing with counselor
- discussing with parents
- thinking of colleges

Categories:
- I visited right number of colleges
- I wish I'd visited more colleges
- Non-involved parents
- Involved parents

Callow Nichols Research Study   Table 1 - 6

#3 When did you Start the College Process?
During Senior Year Summary

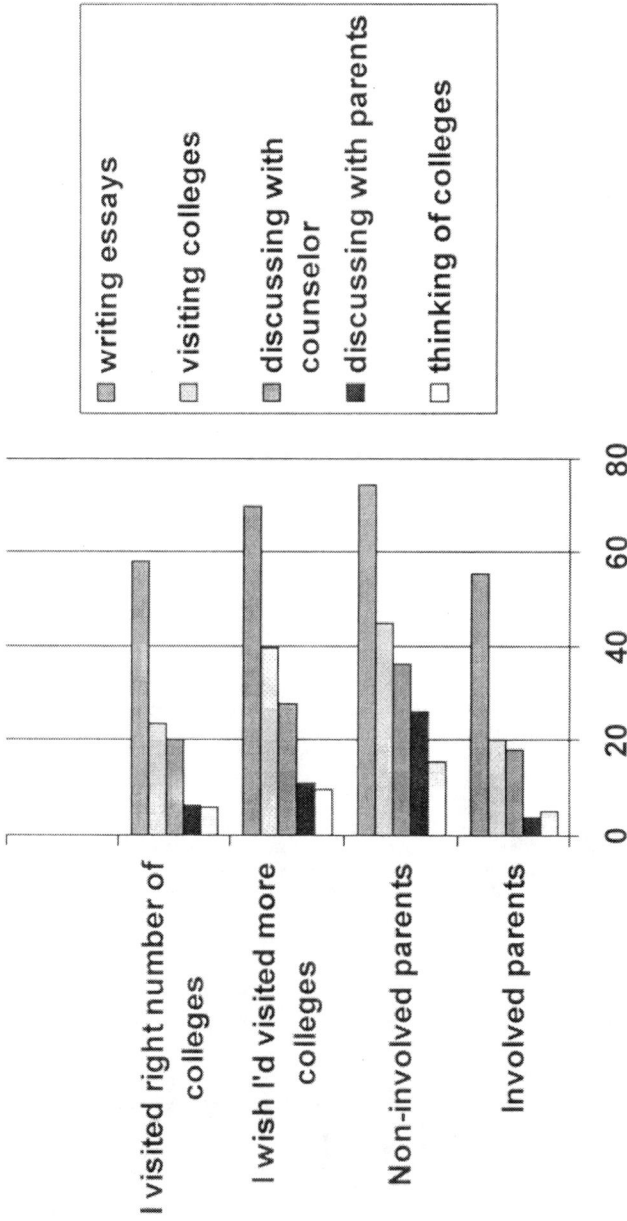

Legend:
- writing essays
- visiting colleges
- discussing with counselor
- discussing with parents
- thinking of colleges

Categories:
- I visited right number of colleges
- I wish I'd visited more colleges
- Non-involved parents
- Involved parents

Callow Nichols Research Study   Table 1 - 10

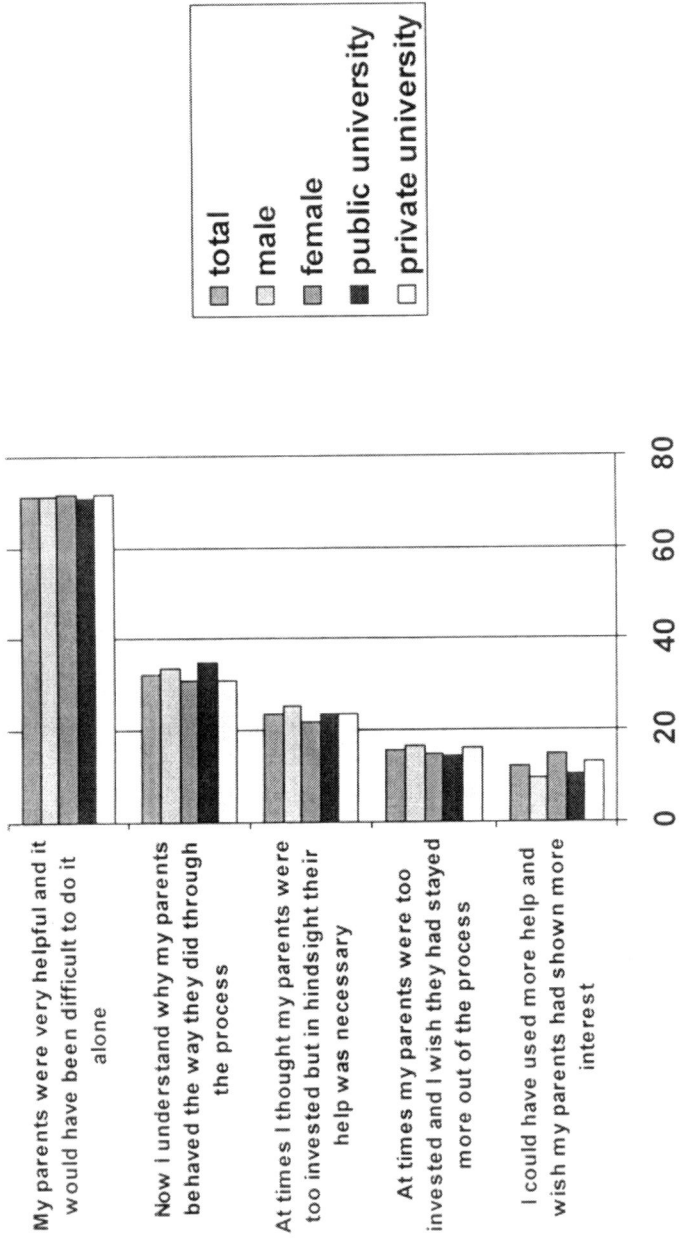

#4 Regarding parental involvement, which applies to you?

Legend:
- total
- male
- female
- public university
- private university

Categories:
- My parents were very helpful and it would have been difficult to do it alone
- Now I understand why my parents behaved the way they did through the process
- At times I thought my parents were too invested but in hindsight their help was necessary
- At times my parents were too invested and I wish they had stayed more out of the process
- I could have used more help and wish my parents had shown more interest

Axis scale: 0, 20, 40, 60, 80

Callow Nichols Research Study.   Table 1 - 60

#5 Regarding parental involvement, which applies to you?

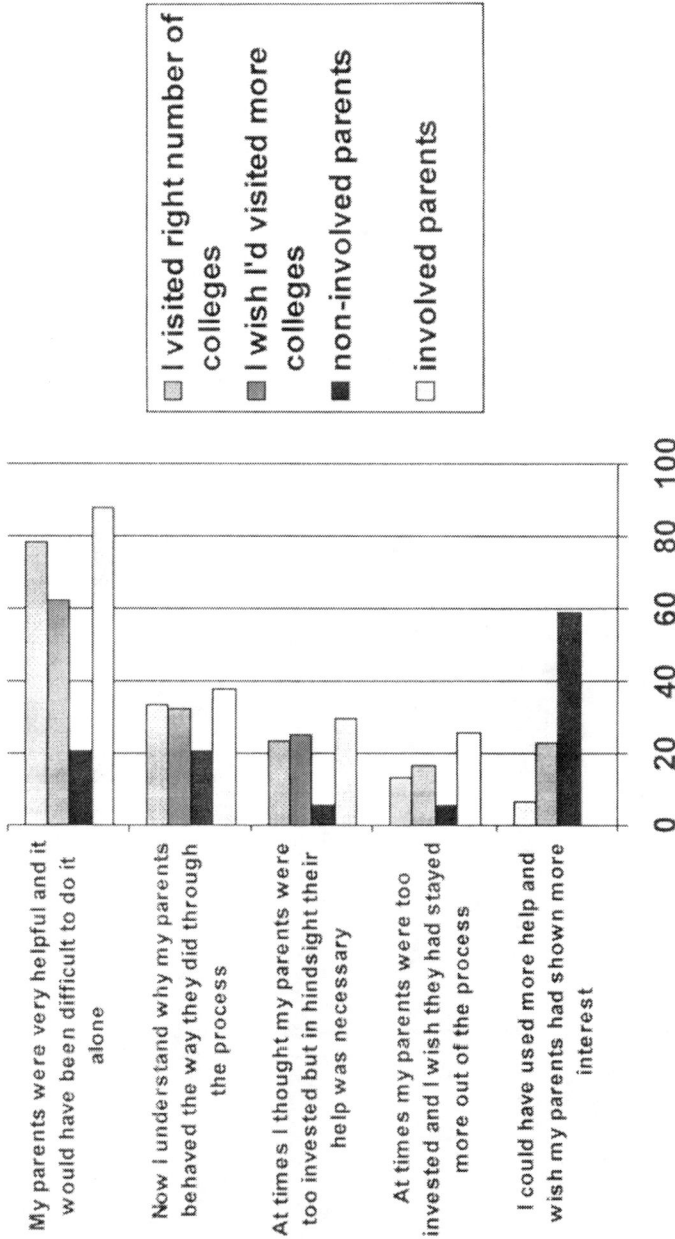

Legend:
- I visited right number of colleges
- I wish I'd visited more colleges
- non-involved parents
- involved parents

Categories:
- My parents were very helpful and it would have been difficult to do it alone
- Now I understand why my parents behaved the way they did through the process
- At times I thought my parents were too invested but in hindsight their help was necessary
- At times my parents were too invested and I wish they had stayed more out of the process
- I could have used more help and wish my parents had shown more interest

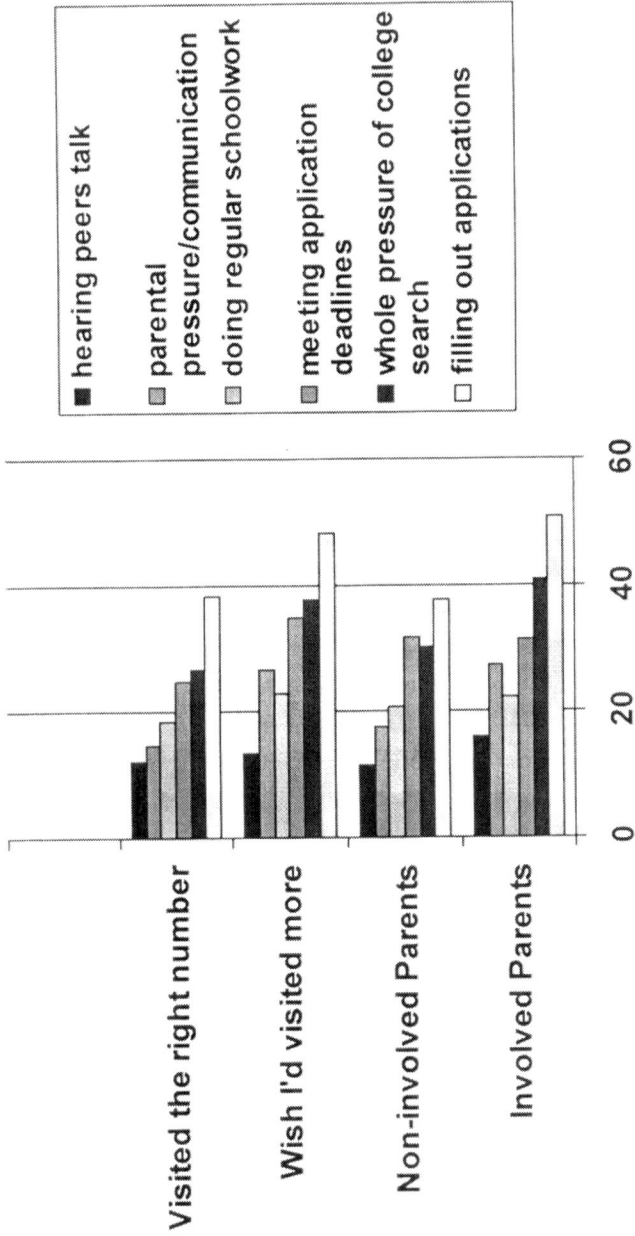

#6 Most Stressful Part of College Application Process (top 2-box summary)

Legend:
- hearing peers talk
- parental pressure/communication
- doing regular schoolwork
- meeting application deadlines
- whole pressure of college search
- filling out applications

Categories: Visited the right number, Wish I'd visited more, Non-involved Parents, Involved Parents

Callow Nichols Research Study   Table 1 - 55

#7 Preparation for Standardized Testing

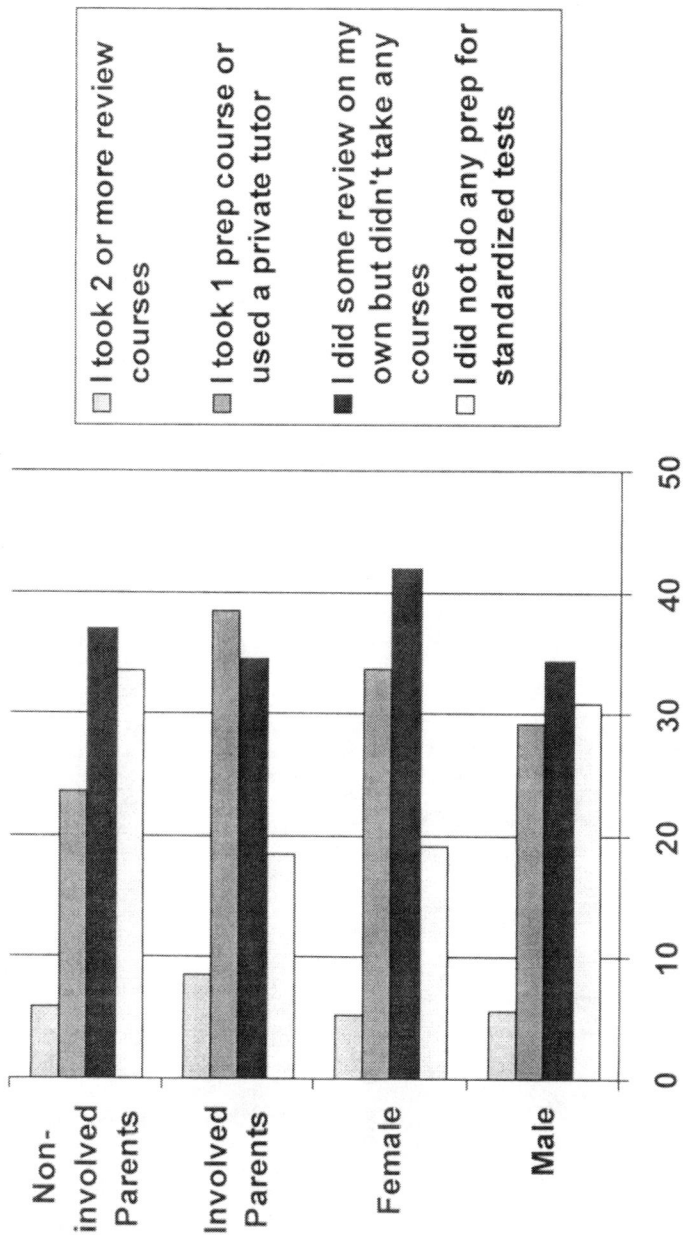

Legend:
- ☐ I took 2 or more review courses
- ▨ I took 1 prep course or used a private tutor
- ■ I did some review on my own but didn't take any courses
- ☐ I did not do any prep for standardized tests

Callow Nichols Research Study   Table 1 - 22

#8 Preparation for Standardized Testing

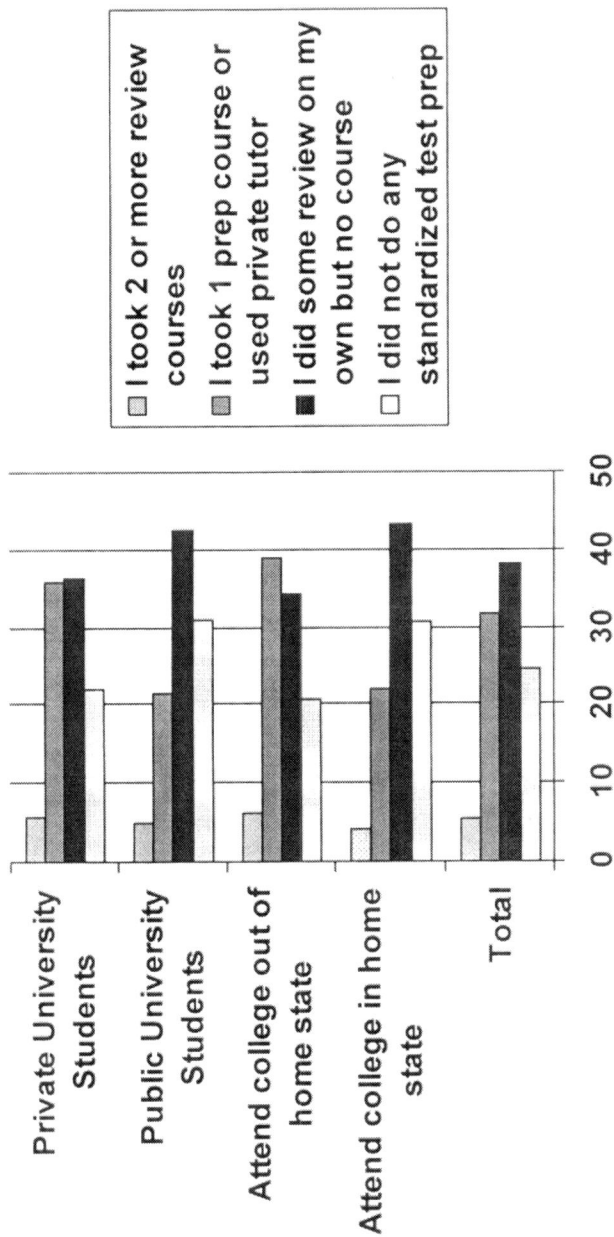

Legend:
- I took 2 or more review courses
- I took 1 prep course or used private tutor
- I did some review on my own but no course
- I did not do any standardized test prep

Categories: Private University Students, Public University Students, Attend college out of home state, Attend college in home state, Total

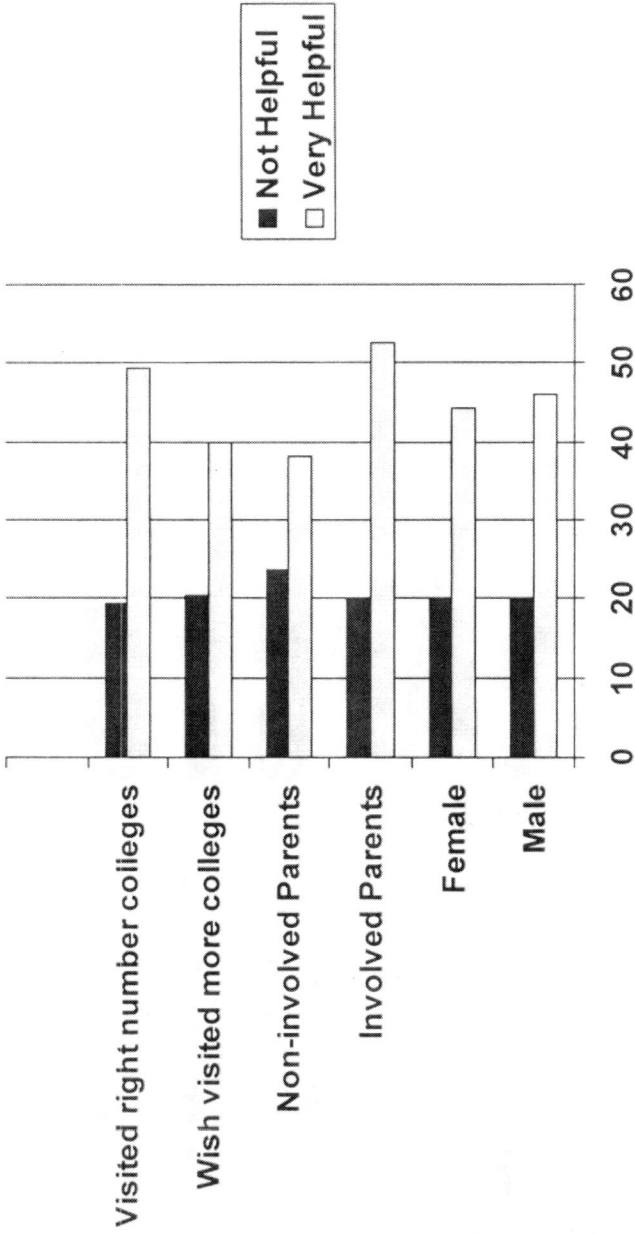

#9 How Helpful was Testing Prep
(top and bottom 2-box)

Legend:
- ■ Not Helpful
- □ Very Helpful

Categories:
- Visited right number colleges
- Wish visited more colleges
- Non-involved Parents
- Involved Parents
- Female
- Male

Callow Nichols Research Study   Table 1 - 23

#10 Effectiveness of Standardized Testing Prep
(top and bottom 2-box summary)

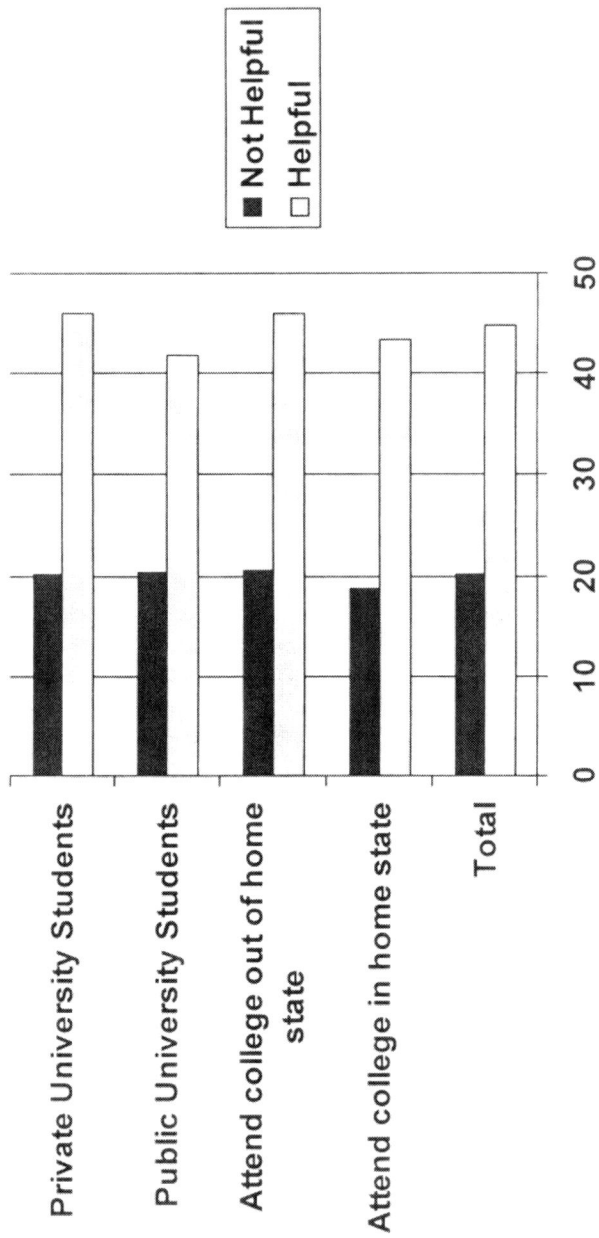

Legend:
- Not Helpful
- Helpful

Categories:
- Private University Students
- Public University Students
- Attend college out of home state
- Attend college in home state
- Total

Callow Nichols Research Study.   Table 2 - 23

#11 Satisfaction with Number of Colleges Visited
(in relation to involvement of parents and number
of colleges applied to)

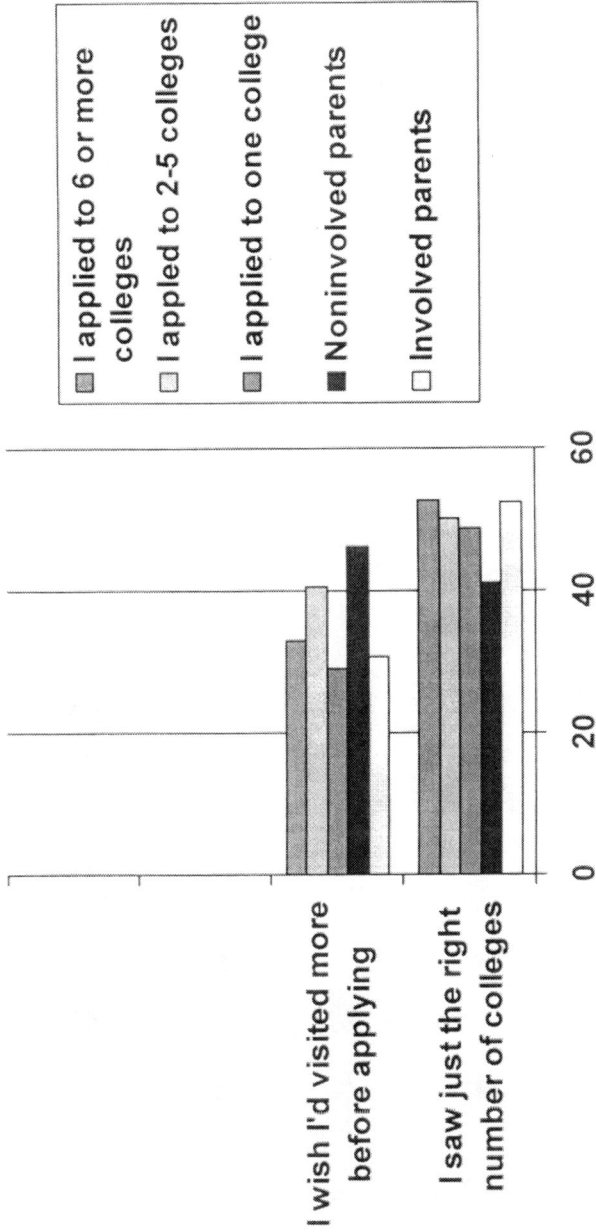

Legend:
- I applied to 6 or more colleges
- I applied to 2-5 colleges
- I applied to one college
- Noninvolved parents
- Involved parents

Categories:
- I wish I'd visited more before applying
- I saw just the right number of colleges

Callow Nichols Research Study   Table 1 - 29

65

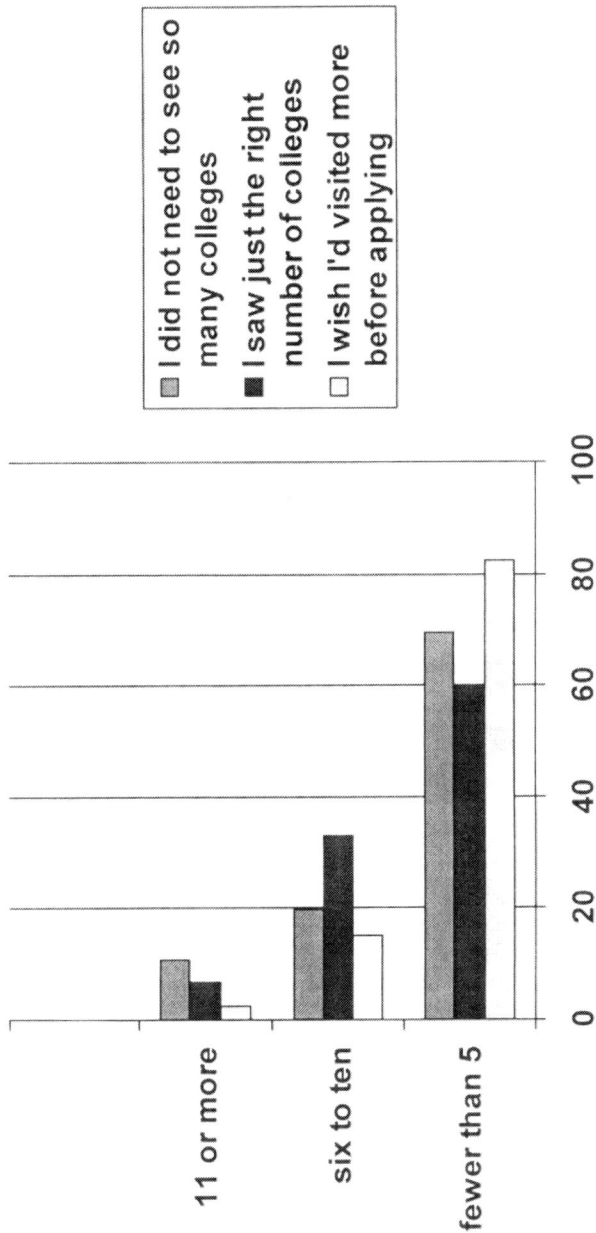

#12 Satisfaction in the Number of Colleges Visited before Applying (in relation to number of colleges visited before applying)

Legend:
- I did not need to see so many colleges
- I saw just the right number of colleges
- I wish I'd visited more before applying

Callow Nichols Research Study   Table 1- 24

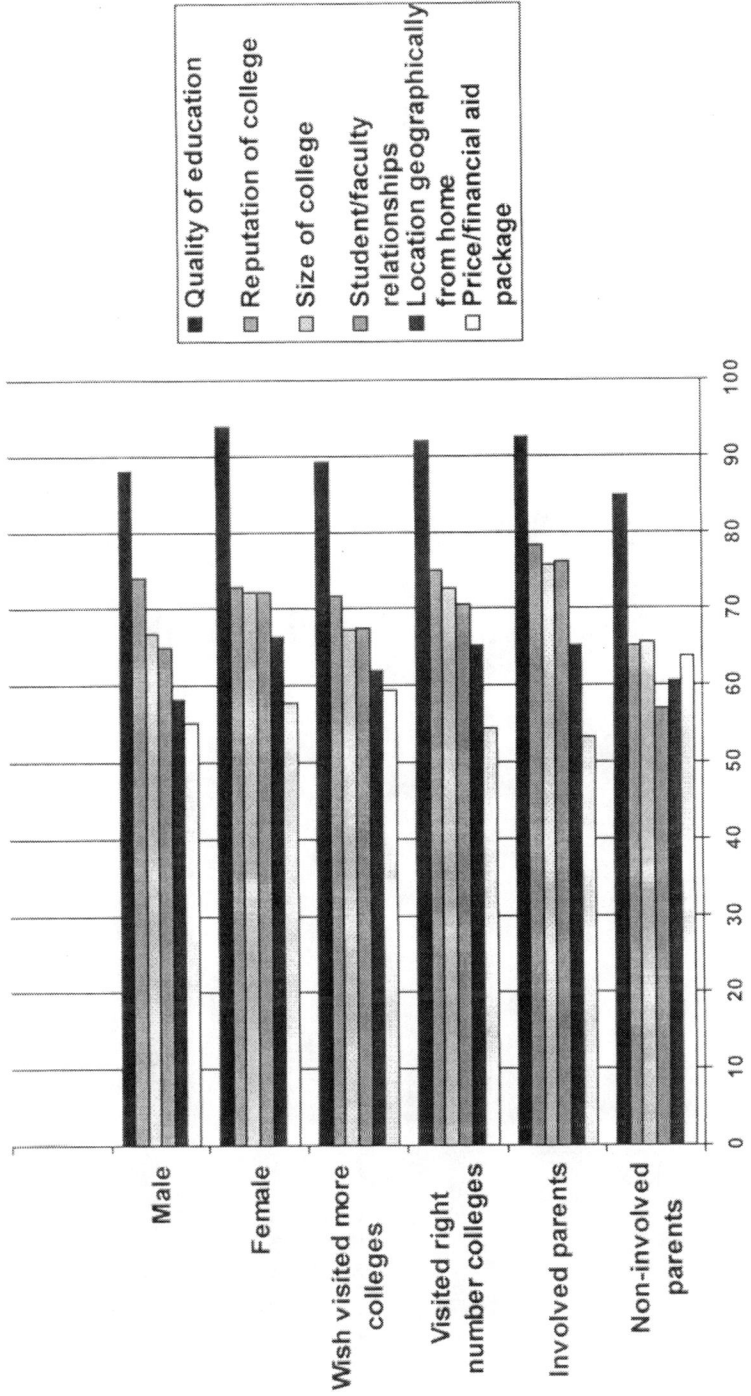

#13 Most Important Reasons I Chose the College I Now Attend (top 2-box summary)

Legend:
- Quality of education
- Reputation of college
- Size of college
- Student/faculty relationships
- Location geographically from home
- Price/financial aid package

Categories: Male, Female, Wish visited more colleges, Visited right number colleges, Involved parents, Non-involved parents

Callow Nichols Research Study   1 - 46

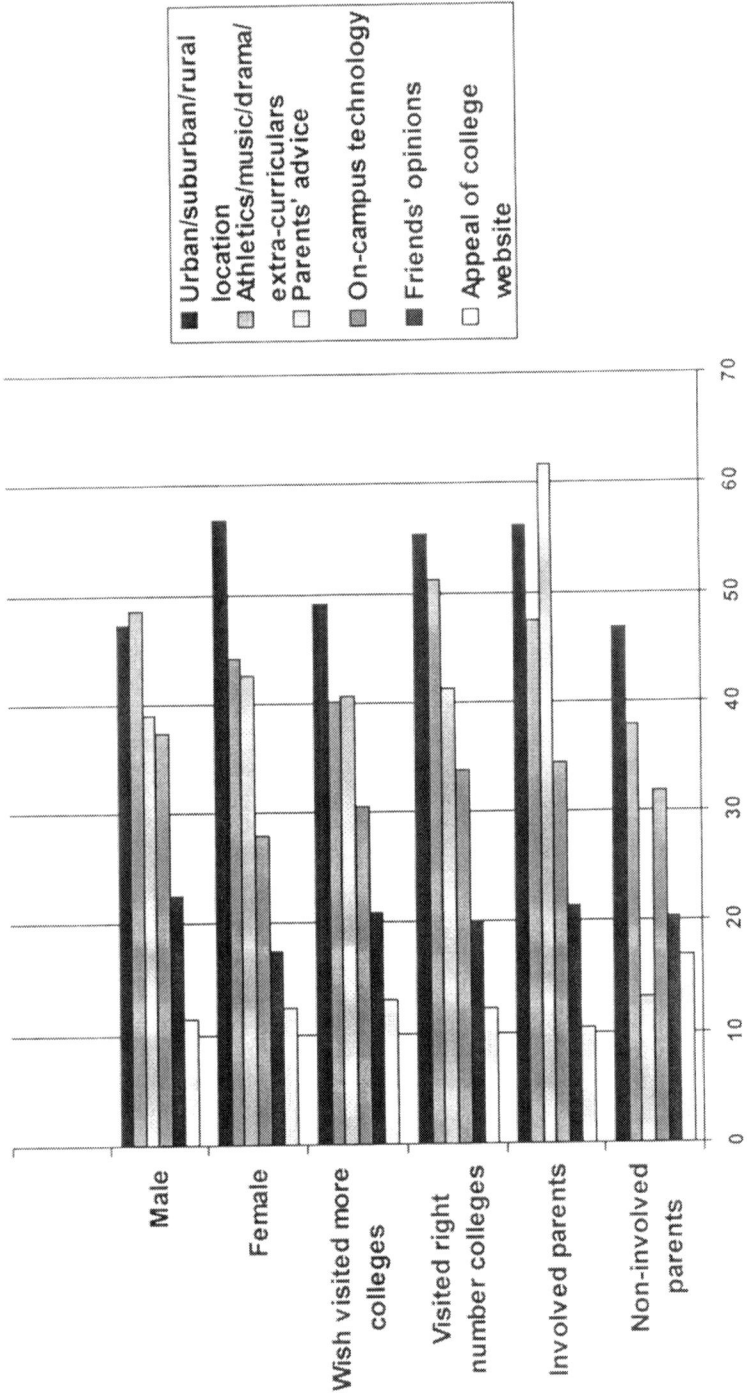

#14 Most Important Reasons I Chose the College I Now Attend (top 2-box summary)

Legend:
- Urban/suburban/rural location
- Athletics/music/drama/extra-curriculars
- Parents' advice
- On-campus technology
- Friends' opinions
- Appeal of college website

Categories: Male, Female, Wish visited more colleges, Visited right number colleges, Involved parents, Non-involved parents

Callow Nichols Research Study   Table 1 - 46

68

#15 Most Important Reasons I Chose the College I Now Attend
(top 2-box summary)

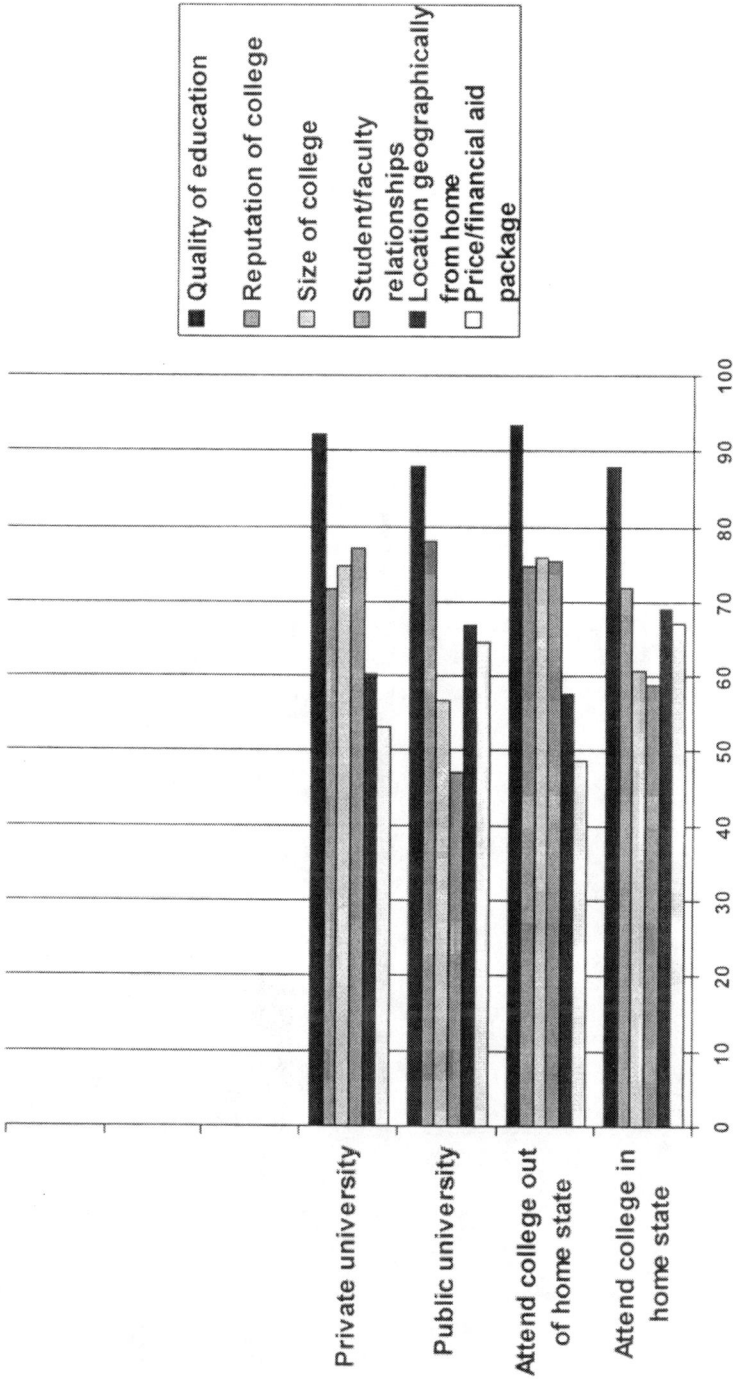

Legend:
- Quality of education
- Reputation of college
- Size of college
- Student/faculty relationships
- Location geographically from home
- Price/financial aid package

Categories:
- Private university
- Public university
- Attend college out of home state
- Attend college in home state

70

#16 Most Important Reasons I Chose the College I Now Attend
(top 2-box summary)

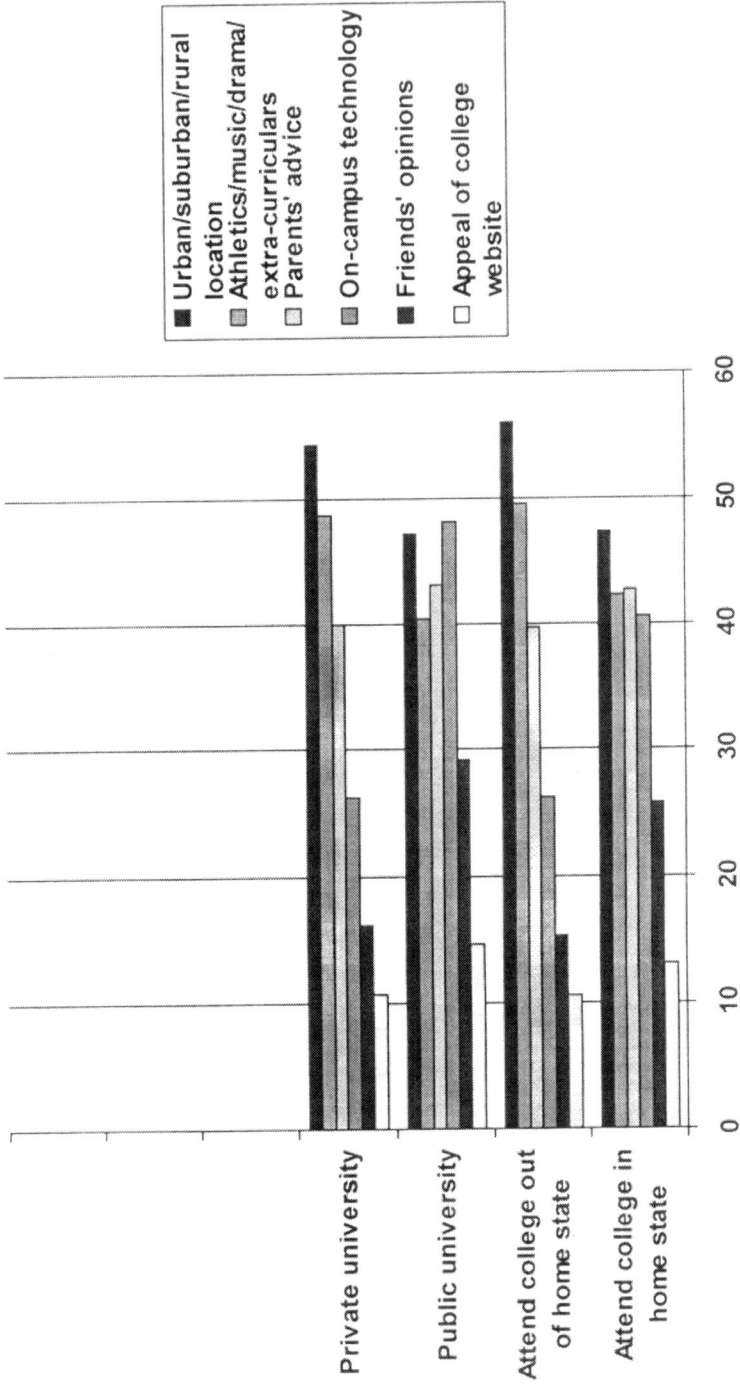

Legend:
- ■ Urban/suburban/rural location
- ▨ Athletics/music/drama/ extra-curriculars
- ▨ Parents' advice
- ▨ On-campus technology
- ■ Friends' opinions
- □ Appeal of college website

Categories:
- Private university
- Public university
- Attend college out of home state
- Attend college in home state

#17 Most Important Reasons I Chose the College I Now Attend
(top 2-box summary)

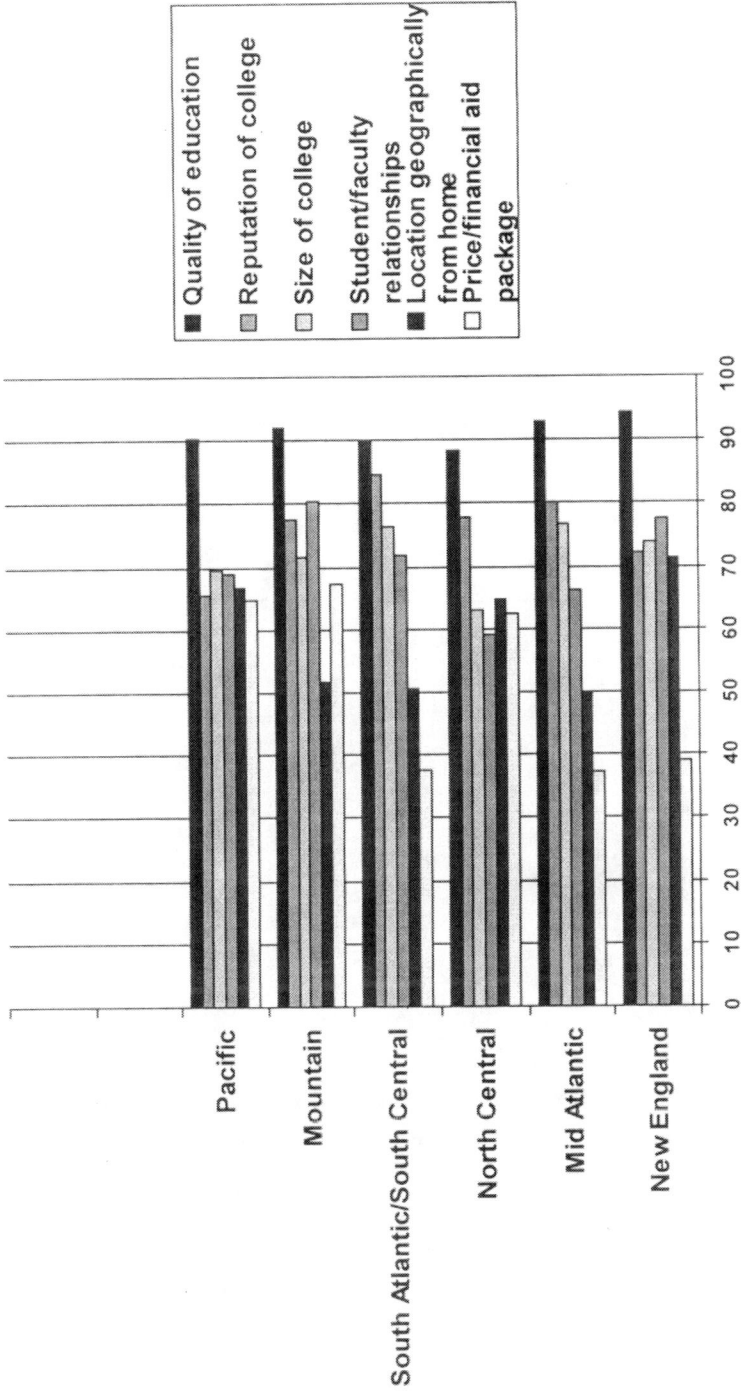

Legend:
- ■ Quality of education
- ▨ Reputation of college
- □ Size of college
- ▥ Student/faculty relationships
- ■ Location geographically from home
- □ Price/financial aid package

Callow Nichols Research Study   Table 2 - 46

#18 Regional Reflection on Parental Involvement

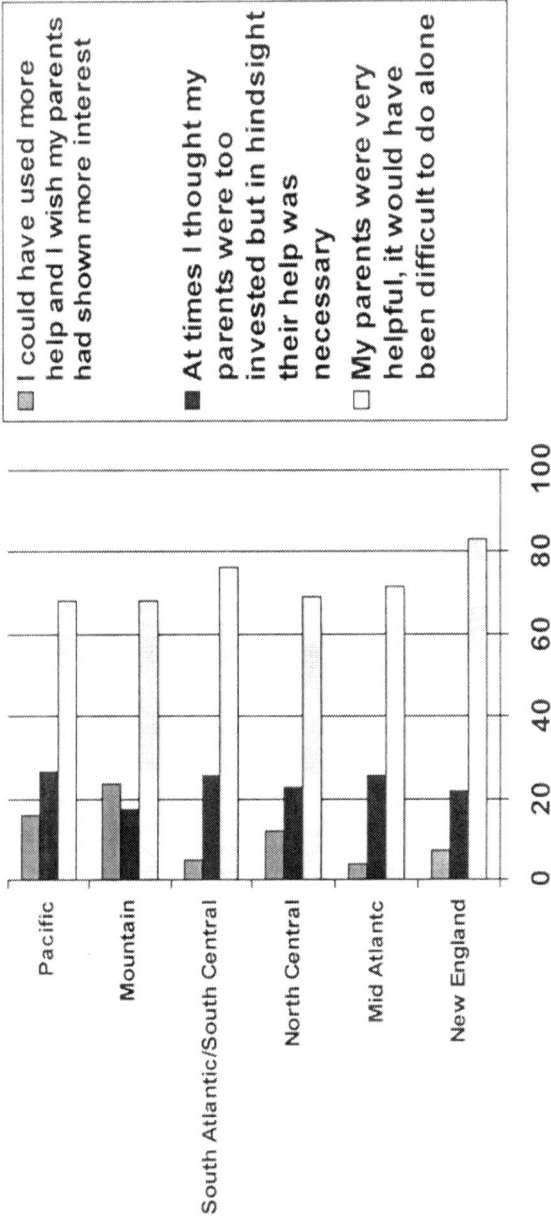

Legend:
- I could have used more help and I wish my parents had shown more interest
- At times I thought my parents were too invested but in hindsight their help was necessary
- My parents were very helpful, it would have been difficult to do alone

Regions: Pacific, Mountain, South Atlantic/South Central, North Central, Mid Atlantc, New England

#19 Satisfaction with the Number of Colleges Visited Before Applying

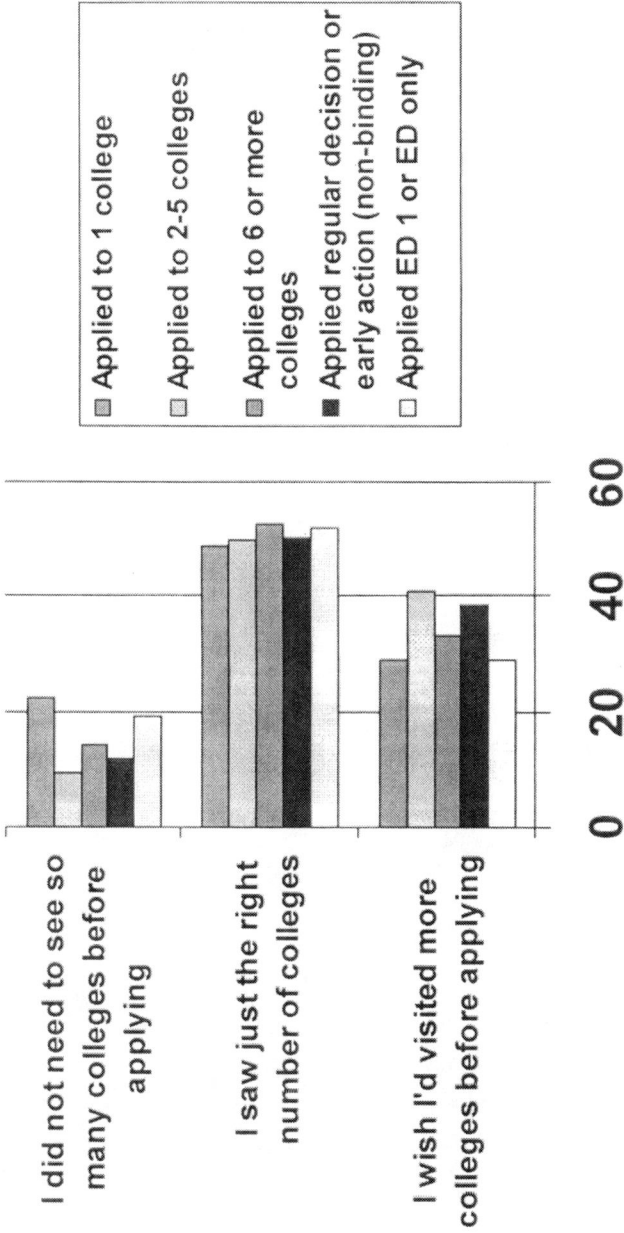

Legend:
- Applied to 1 college
- Applied to 2-5 colleges
- Applied to 6 or more colleges
- Applied regular decision or early action (non-binding)
- Applied ED 1 or ED only

Categories:
- I did not need to see so many colleges before applying
- I saw just the right number of colleges
- I wish I'd visited more colleges before applying

Axis: 0 20 40 60

INDEX

REBECCA CALLOW, a graduate of Wheaton College in Norton, MA, began her professional career in education at the secondary level and has worked with teenagers in coaching and advisory capacities for the last twenty-five years. She has published two children's books: Anthony's Gift and The Marble.

SUSAN NICHOLS had been involved in the college admissions process for over twenty years as a volunteer interviewer and local and national admissions coordinator for Middlebury College in Vermont. She is currently the president of the Middlebury College Alumni Association. In addition, she has worked in market research as a consultant, conducting both qualitative and quantitative research.

Printed in the United States
124435LV00002B/1-324/P